What Greenspan Can't Tell You

What Greenspan Can't Tell You

✦

The Inner Workings of the Investment Markets

Fred Press

iUniverse, Inc.
New York Lincoln Shanghai

What Greenspan Can't Tell You
The Inner Workings of the Investment Markets

iUniverse books may be ordered through booksellers or by contacting:

iUniverse
2021 Pine Lake Road, Suite 100
Lincoln, NE 68512
www.iuniverse.com
1-800-Authors (1-800-288-4677)

Because of the dynamic nature of the Internet, any Web addresses or links contained in this book may have changed since publication and may no longer be valid.

The information, ideas, and suggestions in this book are not intended to render professional advice. Before following any suggestions contained in this book, you should consult your personal accountant or other financial advisor. Neither the author nor the publisher shall be liable or responsible for any loss or damage allegedly arising as a consequence of your use or application of any information or suggestions in this book.

ISBN: 978-0-595-48283-2 (pbk)
ISBN: 978-0-595-60370-1 (ebk)

Printed in the United States of America

Contents

PREFACE

Like the current Chairman of the Federal Reserve (Ben Bernanke), I too have spent a great deal of time studying and analyzing the events surrounding the 1929 stock market crash and the ensuing Great Depression. I have also spent time designing aircraft engines, operating businesses, and "managing" money. I bring to you a wealth of experience from the halls of academia and from the real world.

What Greenspan Can't Tell You is composed of ideas I have accumulated over the course of many years. Some of the ideas and relationships in this book were reduced to paper ten or even twenty years ago (other ideas were beyond the scope of this book and may appear in a future work). The bulk of the text was written in 2005 and the completed manuscript was submitted for copyright protection in March of 2006. The manuscript was slightly updated in May of 2006 to reflect some current events of that time, and remained in that state until now (as tempting as it was to comment on more recent events, I exercised great restraint in order to preserve the integrity of the work). It was edited for typos and syntax in December, 2007, in preparation for publication in 2008. You will be reading this book after January of 2008 (nearly two full years after its original copyright). Some of the events I describe in the book have already played out in the marketplace extraordinarily closely to the way I predicted they would. Many others have not yet occurred because as I outline in the book, the events more or less follow a schedule. The intelligent reader will observe the astonishing accuracy of my forecasts and understand that there is a very high likelihood that those forecasts will continue to be correct. This book was not brought to market sooner, due in part to the time lost in attempting to go through more traditional publishing channels. I apologize for this delay.

I believe the markets are best viewed as a "system" when they are being properly analyzed and discussed. I have therefore meshed certain engineering concepts with business concepts, and applied them together in the analysis and discussion of the "investment markets". You will find these concepts and terminology scattered throughout the book.

I chose to title the book as I did because I believe any chairman of the Federal Reserve must understand the majority of the issues and relationships I discuss throughout the book, but for myriad reasons, is not completely free to discuss those relationships and disclose his true beliefs. Greenspan's name was chosen for inclusion in the title primarily because he was the chairman when I wrote the book and created the title, and because I believe he is largely responsible for our current and future predicaments. I believe that this book will take the reader into any chairman's head and possibly even beyond, in assisting him/her to understand "the inner workings of the investment markets".

My goal in writing the book is to teach the investor much of what I have learned about the investment markets over the course of the last four decades. It is my hope that you will read the book several times, as it contains a wealth of information describing the complex relationships guiding the "investment markets". If you follow my advice and read the book periodically, it should serve as an investing guide for at least the next 30 years. I emphasize reading it a few times because it contains a great deal of information which is difficult to fully absorb in a single reading, and also because distractions from media and other sources will tend to dilute or erase the information presented in this book from your memory, to your detriment.

ACKNOWLEDGEMENTS

I wish to acknowledge my teachers, especially my formative mathematics teachers. And of course, I would like to thank my loved ones for the encouragement given to me as I labored to bring this work to the public.

INTRODUCTION

There are many things that Alan Greenspan (Greenspan) can't tell you about the investment markets, and there are many things your broker or financial advisor (or real estate broker) won't tell you. I phrase things in such a way because I believe that Greenspan understands almost all of what I explain in this book, but unfortunately, he is limited in what he can share with the public. Your broker or financial advisor, however, may understand all of, or some portion of the information in this book, but either way, he/she will share with you only the information he/she would like you to know. It is highly likely that the predominance of information your advisor will share with you will be slanted, and geared to cause you to act in a way that is beneficial to his/her interests.

Generally, the markets of stocks, bonds, cash and their relatives (derivatives) have been referred to in aggregate as the financial markets, distinct from the real estate market. I refer to the financial markets and the real estate market throughout the book as components of the greater "investment markets" (along with gold, art, and other commodities and collectibles), in part because they have become inextricably linked to one another.

The first part of this book summarizes major investment market myths (focusing on the financial and real estate markets), which have been perpetuated by investment market participants over the years. The book then takes the reader into the world of complex relationships which control the financial markets. Real estate, energy, and other issues also receive attention, in an attempt to put all the pieces of the puzzle together so that the reader emerges from the experience with a deeper understanding of the inner workings of the entire system.

Numbers can and do lie, and numbers can be extraordinarily difficult to measure with exact precision. Understanding this, I use only approximate numbers throughout the book, and I am far more concerned with trends rather than attempting to nail down precise figures.

1

GREAT MARKET MYTHS

Myths are created and perpetuated by people. Generally, the people who create and perpetuate those myths typically stand to derive some benefit from them. I have put together some of the greatest investment market myths which are in circulation today. These market myths are not in any particular order of importance, but rather are grouped so that the reader is better able to focus on particular areas of concern. In subsequent areas of this book, we revisit many of these myths and go deeper into the reasons for their existence. In this section, each myth is presented along with an explanation as to why each of them is a myth.

Myth Number One:
They are the professionals and you should listen to them.

Brokers, financial advisors, mutual fund managers, traders, research analysts, and many others may repeat this mantra to the investor over and over in the hopes that it becomes second nature to that investor. When it does become second nature, the investor will have no reason to doubt professional advice, and may be inclined to let someone else manage his/her money. Unfortunately, there's one very big problem with this. These people for the most part cannot be sued for giving bad advice.

Doctors, lawyers, engineers, and tax accountants, among others, can all be sued for malpractice, and this tends to keep them honest. Their disciplines tend to be based on scientific fact or on clear cut rules. The experts on Wall Street (and in the real estate industry) realize that their business is to a large extent a guessing game, as evidenced by the fact that most fund managers are beaten by the market index. There is little science behind their beliefs. Because they rarely say definitively what will happen, they are rarely held accountable when they are wrong. They know this, and because of this, they will tend to do what is in their best interests, not the investor's.

Myth Number Two:
The stock market will go up.

Almost everybody who works in the industry has very good reasons for wanting the stock market to go up. Stock brokers make more money when the market goes up because they get more commissions on trades, and as assets under management grow, they get greater fees for managing more money. Mutual funds, likewise, make more money as the market goes up. And the more the market goes up, the more money the public puts in, further driving assets up, yielding even more fees. Investment bankers want the market to go up because that's when most deals get done, whether it is via mergers and acquisitions or initial public offerings (IPO's). Analysts want the market to go up, because if it goes down, the companies they work for get less fee income, cut costs, and lay off analysts. So whether all these professional market participants realize it or not, at a minimum, subliminally they are wishing the market goes up. And in wishing the market goes up, they begin to believe it will go up. Believing it will go up, they talk it up. This chain of events is perhaps the major force which drives the market to new heights. Add to this that in the vast majority of years, the market does in fact go up, and almost anyone working in the industry would be a fool to talk the market down.

In the other camp are short-sellers ("shorts"), who naturally have an interest in talking the market down. But there are a lot fewer of them, and as can be seen, there are many more people whose livelihoods are completely dependent on the market's growth. Again, whether they realize it or not, people whose livelihoods depend on the market following a particular path will almost always tell an investor that is the path the market will follow.

Myth Number Three:
Efficient market theory works.

I was taught efficient market theory in business school, and I actually believed it for a few years. To summarize, the theory declares that the financial markets are efficient, and the pricing of those markets and of assets in those markets reflects all the information available in the investing universe. It follows then, that an investor cannot outperform the markets, nor can that investor consistently pick out-performing individual securities within those markets. But there is a problem with this theory.

It is incorrect.

While the theory may work when predicting the performance of a random stock will more or less follow that of the broader market, it does not work for predicting the actions of the market, market sectors, or of many individual securities which can fluctuate wildly, and at times can be predicted. As an example, many wise people knew with great certainty that the tech-stock bubble would end in the 1999-2000 timeframe, due to the completion of the year 2000 buildup and the first major phase of the internet build-out. Sadly, proponents of the efficient market theory essentially continue to deny the occurrence of bubbles.

The shortcomings of efficient market theory can be seen when looking at a snapshot in time versus a constantly moving picture. A snapshot of a market at any time will reflect that market as being properly valued in accordance with the efficient market theorists' assumptions that the market reflects all information available at that point in time. However, what the theory does not explain is that the "information" is only the available information at that point in time (i.e. at that snapshot). This "information" does not incorporate the information that can be gleaned from the moving picture (i.e. where things may go in the future and where things have been in the past).

Let's examine what happened in the 1990's to cause the last major stock market bubble. The market was rising rapidly, Greenspan warned of a possible bubble several times, he began to fight it by raising interest rates, but when he almost destabilized the markets (Long Term Capital Management, Russia and all emerging markets), he backed off and lowered rates, further fueling the bubble. He feared raising rates again due to the approaching Y2K (Year 2000) issue, which, combined with huge technology investments in addressing Y2K and the internet build-out, caused revenues (and in many cases profits) of companies to rise rapidly. All these forces came together to fuel the tech bubble. As the economy got past Y2K without a major problem, Greenspan realized he had a final chance to lift interest rates to pop the bubble which had been growing for several years.

All along the way, if one had taken snapshots at moments in time, the argument could have been made that there was no bubble, as in each case market valuations were supported by various metrics being used to justify the value of those markets. However, backing away from each snapshot and putting all available information together into a moving picture, one can see that the bubble existed and was recognized, but until late 1999/2000, not much was able to be done about it, for fear of causing a world-wide catastrophe which might have been brought on by the Y2K issue. The efficient market theorists are correct at each moment frozen in time, but the real world does not work as moments frozen in time. The world and its markets work as moving, evolving phenomena, and this is what allows a bubble to form in the first place.

Many metrics have been used in recent years to value markets, such as number of eyeballs, revenue, profit, P/E (price-to-earnings ratio), P/BV (price to book value), P/S (price-to-sales ratio), enterprise value, earnings yield of a market compared to Treasury yields, and any of a multitude of different ratios and formulas. The funny thing about these various metrics is that they can be used to support a market's fair value at any snapshot in time using efficient market theory, while the moving picture reveals that there are forces which have coerced and/or assisted the markets in getting to their lofty points. Looked at another way, "beauty is in the eye of the beholder", or applied to the markets, the efficient market theorists have taken their market, frozen it in time, and dressed it up in their valuation metrics so that they actually believe (and/or would have the investor believe) it is appropriately valued. Efficient market theory is by its own design, never wrong, which is absurd, and in fact suggests that it can rarely be right.

The markets are a reflection of everything that the universe of market participants collectively understand and emote. They behave not that differently than living organisms. They live off greed, fear, hope, and myths. They cannot be tamed. The best they can be is managed. And those who understand how they are managed are in a position to outperform the average investor.

Myth Number Four:
After the stock market bubble burst, billions of dollars "evaporated".

This myth is perhaps the cruelest of them all. If the professionals can get the less sophisticated investor to believe this one, then they can count on the investor coming back for more. The myth of "evaporation" is a marketing concept, which is nothing more than psychological warfare.

Money does not "evaporate". Paper money can be torn into shreds or burned, but it does not "evaporate". Coins and bullion can be melted and reconstituted, or buried, but they do not "evaporate". Just as the first law of thermodynamics explains the "conservation of energy", so too is there the "conservation of money" (or "conservation of wealth"). In present day society, when we refer to "money", we are really talking about "wealth". Energy and wealth are not destroyed or evaporated, but rather they are both transferred, in accordance with natural and man-made laws, respectively. Energy is transferred into another form, and wealth is simply transferred to other people (but never "evaporated").

To the poor fool who bought at the top of the market, it may feel as though his money evaporated, and believing that his money evaporated (affecting everybody else in the process as well) may help to ease his pain, but it is simply not true. The reality is that the investment banks made their money on IPO's and other deals, almost all of their employees kept their gargantuan bonuses from the bull market years, the executives of public companies kept or cashed out of millions of shares of stock, and many of the traders made out on the way up and on the way down. Sadly, the reality is that the term "evaporate" only applies to the poor fool who bought at or near the top. And can we blame the industry for wanting to allow us to believe that everyone lost money when it "evaporated"? Perhaps if small investors believe that the money really "evaporated", then they would believe that everyone lost money, and they won't be as angry at their advisors and money managers.

Many intelligent people I know have a difficult time understanding this concept, so an example should help to clarify. I know someone who manufactures overseas and imports his goods for sale in the US. When I explained the "evaporation" myth to him several years ago, he failed to understand why it was a myth. To help explain my concept to him, I gave a scenario in which he pays to have a shipping container full of goods shipped to the US. When the container arrives, and he opens it, he finds that the container is empty. After investigating what might have happened, he realizes that somewhere between the manufacturing facility and the US port, the goods were stolen. His money is gone and his goods are gone. He knows little else, but one thing he does know for certain is that his goods and his money did not "evaporate". His goods were transferred to someone else in accordance with the law of the "conservation of wealth".

Myth Number Five:
It's not timing the market; it's time in the market.

If I had ten dollars for every time I heard someone make this statement, I believe I could have retired long ago. The most common argument supporting this myth goes something like "if you missed the 30 days of biggest market gains over the years, then you would have missed half of the total market move over that period". The goal, of course is to get the investor to put a substantial portion of his/her money into the market, and to leave it there for several decades. But what the advisor never tells the investor is that if he/she had missed the 30 days of largest losses, that investor would have handily out-performed the stock market.

Don't believe this "time in the market" nonsense. An investor's goal should be to get out of the market when it is greatly overvalued, and to get into the market when it is greatly undervalued.

Myth Number Six:
You can't time the market so invest for the long term.

This myth is closely related to myth number five, but its importance necessitates its own categorization. In general, the more money investors have in the market, the more money advisors and money managers can make on fees. But there is another extremely important reason the pros need investors' money in the market for the long term. I refer to this as "BALLAST".

The huge amount of investor money in the market for the long term acts as ballast, or as a stabilizing force. Knowing that less sophisticated investors have been convinced to keep their money in the market for the long haul, the pros can count on a certain "floor" to the market. It is highly unlikely the market would go beneath this floor, and this is what enables the pros themselves to time the market. The successful ones can run up huge profits, selling at tops and buying at bottoms. While the pros make their money, small investors stay the course, and in aggregate, at best, match the S&P500 index. If the reader understands the relationship I described, then he/she should come to the realization that many people are successfully timing the market, usually at the expense of the less sophisticated investor.

There are many reasons investors are told to buy for the long term. Clearly, the pros would like the investor in the market for the long term so that they can earn more fees, and also, use investor money as ballast for their own trading. Putting these issues aside, there was a time when there might have been a good reason to buy for the long term, but those days are long gone. Before discount brokers came along and started undercutting the big boys, it could cost several hundred dollars to place a 100-share trade. In the past, if an investor were lucky or skilled enough to actually make money on a trade, his/her gains could be completely wiped out by trading costs. Obviously, in such a situation, one should hold onto a position and allow gains to accumulate to the point where the gain dwarfs the trading costs incurred in making that gain. But this is no longer the situation, so there is really no reason for this particular strategy other than for tax considerations.

Currently, an investor can trade 1000 shares of stock for about $10 at discount brokerages like Fidelity, Schwab, and Vanguard (and a host of others), and as this cost gets lower, one should expect to see much greater turnover in ownership of stocks, as market participants seek to capitalize on ever-smaller movements in stock prices.

Myth Number Seven:
Any intelligent person can be a successful day trader.

This myth is a favorite of the day trading firms, who hope to lure unsuspecting candidates to use their services (for a fee, of course). There are particular times that anyone can be a successful day trader, and skill has nothing to do with it. There are other times that the smartest person in the world cannot be a successful day trader, and bad luck has everything to do with it. Let's analyze what is often happening in the business of day trading.

The Wall Street firms and many trading companies have intensive computer programs along with records of all types of historical data that are continuously fed into their computers. Computer programs sort the data to come up with hourly, daily, weekly, monthly, quarterly, annual, and seasonal trends for markets, sectors, stocks within particular industries for large-caps, mid-caps, small-caps, and IPO's, as well as bonds, gold, and you name it. Over time, a less sophisticated investor cannot beat them at this game. They simply have too much fire power. To go up against these pros in day trading is like going to war with a musket to face off against an enemy with a machine gun. An investor might, however, be very successful in the short term, as long as the market is going his/her way. The down side to this, of course, is that he/she may become deluded into believing that he/she is a great day trader and will set himself/herself up for a massive loss when the market reverses course. Even if the investor is making money, he/she will still underperform the pros, because he/she does not have access to the same firepower they use. Of particular concern are the offers from discount brokerage firms which lower the cost to trade as one does more trades. This can have the undesired effect of turning an investor into a day trader, and in the process, make that investor vulnerable. The brokerage firm will do well, because even though the investor's cost per trade is lower, it will make more money from increased trading volume.

I liken day trading to a man tossing a coin. For argument's sake, let's assume the chances of guessing the correct direction of a stock for a day trade are 50-50, just as it is for calling a coin toss. Now let's assume a man tosses a coin 100 times in a month and comes up with 60 "heads" and 40 "tails", after predicting similar results. He might believe that he is a skilled coin tosser. He might be inclined to bet someone that he can repeat this feat. But he knows better. He knows that the likelihood is that the next 100 tosses will come up 50-50. Perhaps maybe even 40-60, rather than 60-40. He also realizes that if he tosses 1000 times, chances are even greater that he will come out 50-50 (in this case 500-500). He also realizes that he doesn't have to pay anybody for the privilege of tossing a coin as he does with trading. If a rational person understands this, then why would this same person believe that he can do better than 50-50 as a day trader when he is going up against the pros with their arsenal of weaponry?

Myth Number Eight:
Hedge funds are the new elixir.

Hedge funds are the new elixir, and they will make you lots of money and/or keep you from losing money.

Sounds too good to be true, doesn't it?

Ah, the wonderful world of hedge funds. What a place to be to make money—that is if you run the hedge fund.

Since there is virtually no regulation of the hedge fund industry and many funds fly under the radar, there is no way to know their true overall performance figures. It is estimated that only 40 to 50% of hedge funds out-perform the major indexes on a consistent basis. Further, the ones that don't are continuously closed down, and many are reopened under new management (sometimes even the same management). It is a world of the old boy network, where people who control a lot of money give it to their friends and former colleagues to manage (they usually do not give much of their own money, however, and that should tell the reader something). What is evident is that the people running the hedge funds make lots of money for themselves. They typically collect a one to two percent management fee, and then keep 20% of the funds' returns (and these are not necessarily realized returns).

For the best take on what the hedge fund industry is all about, think back to 1998 when the geniuses of Long Term Capital Management would have lost everything had they not been bailed out in a deal orchestrated by the Federal Reserve. And if they could fail, then any fund using margin, derivatives, or shorting techniques can also fail.

Myth Number Nine:
We're only in the early stages of a market recovery.

It's amazing to find financial industry professionals who profess that the markets are always in the "early innings" of a recovery, and who instruct their clients to put more money into those markets. It's as if they believe that 2000-2003 was just a blip along a 50-year run, or even worse, that early 2003 was the start of a period of uninterrupted gains that will last 20 years.

As an example, in 2005, many professionals argued that the stock market still had a long way to go, coming off its bottom of early 2003. But those same pros often failed to mention that the average recovery lasts only two years. They also neglected to mention that the markets had already risen over 50% during this recovery, which just so happened to be the typical gain during the typical two-year recovery period. Nor did they say that valuations were priced to perfection. They had no idea if interest rates would continue to go up, what might happen in Iraq, Iran, or North Korea, nor with Al Qaeda, and/or bird flu, nor with China trade issues, just to name a few things. After the typical run-up in the stock market, those advisors really should have been warning their clients of the poor risk/return climate going forward.

As they instruct their clients to put more money into the stock market, there is one thing that virtually no money manager will do, and that is provide an audited statement showing what percent of their personal wealth is allocated to the stock market at various points in time, so that investors can see if their advisors and money managers practice what they preach.

Myth Number Ten:
Options and other "protection" techniques are good for you.

For the investor who is hesitant to buy stocks and other assets, Wall Street has created an area of mystique known as hedging strategies. Wall Street has actually managed to convince investors that by purchasing hedging products, investors can protect themselves. But I caution that before buying, investors should ask themselves whether the brokerage firms would really bother to spend all their time and energy on these products if they weren't confident that they would be the ones who come out ahead. It is important to recall here, the law of "conservation of wealth".

And how do the pros come out ahead? They come out ahead at the expense of the less knowledgeable investor. First, the firms make money through transaction fees. Second, because the average investor can't possibly compete with all their data and number crunching firepower, they make money using these strategies at the investors' expense in the marketplace. My advice is to forget all these hedging gimmicks and to make money the old fashioned way.

Remember, the Nobel laureates at Long Term Capital incorporated all sorts of hedging strategies, and even they would have ended up in the poorhouse had not the Fed come to their rescue. Also remember, that if a small investor gets into trouble with hedging strategies, the Fed will not be coming to that investor's rescue.

Myth Number Eleven:
The Inflation Index is accurate.

I believe that the inflation index numbers put out by the government are not to be taken seriously. Three of the greatest forces of inflation which almost everybody experiences—housing, education and healthcare—are not properly reflected in the index, and the cost of food and energy are "managed". Health insurance is going up over 10% per year, college education has risen over 7% per year, the cost of New York City public transportation and taxi's recently jumped anywhere from 20 to 35%, a slice of pizza went up $.25, soon everyone will have to pay for cable television (which itself has gone up over 5% per year for a decade) to watch just the most basic channels, and let's not forget the cost of energy. All this, and somehow the inflation rate for the last few years has averaged about 3% or less!

Apparently, because we can now play better videogames on a computer and watch television (TV) on a large, flat-panel screen, we have done away with inflation.

Apparently the government has decided that these luxuries which we don't need are driving down the inflationary effects of the things we do need, like energy (heat, electricity, air conditioning, and gasoline), health care, education, and housing.

I estimate the real inflation rate of the last few years to be over 5% per year versus the stated rate of 3% and less. But why is this? I will never claim to completely understand why things are as they are, but I do have a few explanations as to why they may be so. I believe that the first reason for the low stated inflation rate is that the stock market had crashed in 2000, and economic theory has shown that to avoid a deflationary spiral and depression following such a crash, interest rates need to be very low. The low rates encourage lots of spending and investment by business and consumers, which gets the economy going again. If numbers can show that there is no inflation, then interest rates can be held at extremely low levels. Another reason for the low stated inflation rate may be because the government uses the inflation index to determine how much it increases it's payments for things like Medicare, Medicaid, Social Security, wages and benefits for all levels of government employees, rates for all classes of government contractors and so on, as all these payments are generally indexed to inflation in some form. In a high deficit situation, it would naturally be very desirable for the government to keep as much money as possible in its coffers, and one way of achieving this goal could be by keeping the stated inflation rate low.

Yet another reason for the low stated inflation rate could be the phenomenon of self-fulfilling prophesy. Generally, when everyone believes inflation is increasing, inflation increases. What occurs in such a climate is that businesses raise their prices to stay ahead of or to keep up with their costs, workers make stronger demands for compensation increases, and consumers make rapid purchases before prices can rise even higher. Such activity fuels inflation even more until there is a full-blown inflation crisis. If the government can maintain a low inflation rate, even if it is an artificially low inflation rate, the economy can actually be "tricked" into believing there is no inflation or that there is extremely low inflation, which itself can become a self-fulfilling prophesy. This would then encourage businesses, workers, and consumers to go on with business as usual. The desired end result would be little or no inflation. The reader, however, should understand the reality that his/her dollars have been eaten away by inflation at an average rate of about 5% per year for the past few years.

Myth Number Twelve:
The Productivity Index accurately measures productivity.

I do not believe that US productivity has been as high as the reported numbers would suggest. To make a determination as to how accurate the index may be, one needs to first consider what goes into GDP (Gross Domestic Product). Think about all the hedge funds, mutual funds, private-equity funds, insurance companies, and other finance companies or finance arms of companies which are essentially just moving money around from entity to entity, with no real "production" to show for it, and all the time while doing so, generating huge fees. I don't understand which of these numbers shows up in the calculations, and I don't know if anyone really does. The net result, of course, could be the appearance that the US economy is producing more with less. Consider that following the implosion of the stock market bubble in 2000, it was revealed that approximately 30% of packaged software which had been sold during the bubble was still sitting on shelves, unwrapped, and likely never to be used. It was also revealed that 97% of the capacity of fiber optic cable which had been laid might never be used. Yet all this purchased software and laid fiber optic cable was counted in the alleged productivity boom.

The government has an interest in showing that the economy is more productive than it is. By showing that productivity goes up, even as employment rises, the government can support its claim that inflation is lower than it truly is. I believe that when the government shows inflation is low and productivity is high, it is hoping to "trick" the economy into believing these things, and therefore create self-fulfilling prophesies of low inflation and high productivity. However, if enough participants in the economy refused to believe the government's numbers, then the economy would run the risk of a self-fulfilling inflation problem. It is very possible that the government's job has become to manage the "perception" of productivity, and hence, inflation, rather than the reality of productivity and inflation.

Myth Number Thirteen:
Information technology allows companies to better forecast and plan ahead.

Provided a company truly has an outstanding information technology system which allows it to forecast coming events, it might have an advantage over its competitors, but only if those competitors have far inferior systems. Yet, very often, even with all their technology, companies don't see what is fast approaching. I still remember when the CEO (Chief Executive Officer) of a major technology company publicly stated in early 2000 that he did not see any changes in the business climate ahead.

In the event product demand starts to slow, companies seek to maintain market share. In doing so, competition forces them to offer more goods or services for less money. It doesn't even matter much that a company may be able to see a slowdown coming, because once that slowdown has come, that company has no choice but to do what it can to keep market share. Maintaining market share comes in the form of price and/or profit decreases. Eventually, none of the competing companies are making much money, until whatever caused the problem in the first place is corrected. But at that point, the damage is done, as the pros have fled from the stocks of these companies.

Myth Number Fourteen:
CEO's must be paid extraordinary compensation.

Many claim that CEO's of large public corporations must be paid wages which are 500 times those of the average employee at those corporations. Such claims are utter nonsense. In reality, there is no shortage of qualified executives that would do just as well as the current ones for compensation only 50 times the average employee's wages.

The real reason such outlandish compensation occurs is that the old boys club is alive and well. CEO's sit on each other's boards and are members of the same clubs, and they would like to keep it that way. I view the net result as what I jokingly refer to as "compensation fixing". Each time a CEO of one company gets an unbelievable compensation package, the ante is raised for all the others to get the same.

It's always been difficult for me to believe that the CEO of a company is worth so much more than the critical people who are able to do things that no CEO is even capable of doing. I often hear people on TV and in other places defending the outrageous compensation packages earned by many CEO's and other executives. An argument I've heard many times is an analogy that someone like Tiger Woods, who is by far the best in his game, earns whatever the market will pay, so CEO's should be entitled to similar rewards, since they are the best at their games. But those CEO's should not be entitled to such huge sums for a very good reason. Tiger Woods has shown himself to be the best, period. He and his opponents compete on an open playing field while a world-wide audience can observe their every move, and when a winner emerges, there is no question of who he is and how he got there. Tiger's dominance rests solely on his ability to vanquish his opponents on a completely opaque playing field. While the CEO unquestionably vanquishes his opponents, this is not necessarily what makes a great CEO. One can make a very valid argument that the people who might make the best CEO's are the ones that never even occupy the office of CEO. The winner of the CEO contest is usually determined by a host of factors, among them, loyalty, cunning, legacy, and contacts, in addition to the assumed intelligence, stamina, street smarts, book smarts, and team building and leadership skills, among others.

In the world of golf there is one Tiger Woods and a few runners-up who make huge sums of money. In the world of business, there are thousands who make these huge and outlandish sums of money. I seriously question whether so many CEO's possess the relative skill of Tiger Woods. I also seriously question that any CEO of a large, public company is irreplaceable.

Myth Number Fifteen:
As long as we have low interest rates, real estate values will rise.

In the 1970's and 1980's, the prevailing wisdom was that real estate would rise as a hedge against the inflation of those times. Of course, interest rates were high in that era in order to combat inflation. How odd that lately the prevailing talk has been that real estate would rise with low inflation and low interest rates. My understanding is that the arguments for real estate in low interest rate and high interest rate environments are opposing arguments, yet both have been used by the real estate bulls to push values higher. Using this type of thinking, the bull market should never end, which is ludicrous.

Many areas of the US experienced a surge in real estate values in the 1980's which was followed by a crash, and the US market has now had a surge in the

2000's, which will also likely end in a crash. The reality is that an important reason real estate values were continuing to go up as of 2005 was because low interest rates (along with new and ever-increasing exotic financing vehicles) had made mortgages more affordable. This, of course, is a double-edged sword, as the cost of real estate has risen with lower interest rates and exotic mortgages, making this same real estate less affordable. Sadly, as inflation and interest rates continue to rise, there will be no one left to afford the high-priced real estate, causing a collapse in prices to compensate for the higher interest rates.

There was not a massive run-up in real estate prices in the 1960's during the benign interest rate environment at that time (at odds with the current boom), which left a lot of upside for the 70's and 80's. That latter period had the added advantage of a massive changeover from one wage-earner to two wage-earner households, which helped fuel rising real estate prices. By the 1990's, the US had already experienced this demographic shift, and in the future cannot rely on a greater percentage of two wage-earner households to drive continued price increases.

Myth Number Sixteen:
Real estate prices have never declined year-over-year, nationally.

People who earn their livelihoods from real estate love to perpetuate this myth in the hope that it becomes a self-fulfilling prophesy, going forward. Sadly, it is a false statement.

While it may be true that average nationwide real estate prices have not declined year-over-year recently, when taking inflation into account, they declined significantly in the early 1980's, and did so again in the early 1990's. There is, in fact, a long, world-wide history of real estate declines. In the case of hyper-growth markets, there are very real risks of drops in real value of over 50%.

As an example, assume you bought a condo in New York City in 2005 for $1 million, and over the next 7 years it falls in value by 25% to $750 thousand. Not that terrible? If you put that $1 million into a municipal money market fund which might pay an average of 5% over that 7-year period, you would earn nearly 40% with compounded interest, largely tax-free. This missed gain (often referred to as an opportunity cost) of 40% and your loss of 25% add up to a very serious loss. Of course, in all fairness, this analysis doesn't take into account the rent which a homeowner might otherwise have to pay or the benefits of mortgage interest tax credits (which may not last for much longer anyway), but nor does it take into account real estate taxes, home maintenance costs, nor a slew of other personal and individual issues which need to be evaluated. It also doesn't take into account that people tend to rent less expensive space than they purchase in an upwardly trending market, and therefore might have far lower carrying costs by renting. The bottom line is that you can get badly burned in real estate, and I know many intelligent people who did in the late 1980's and early 1990's.

To convey the seriousness of the current situation, it is of the utmost importance to note that the US national market did experience a very significant, multi-decade real decline in home values in the first half of the 20th century, which is rarely sited by anyone in the industry.

Myth Number Seventeen:
Home prices can't collapse because everybody needs to live somewhere.

Let's take a close look at this fantasy put out there by the realtors and their friends. Compare some local bubbles (New York City, California, Florida, Washington, DC, Las Vegas, and Boston) to the tech stocks in 2000 or even to General Motors (GM) in 2005 or the stock market in 1987. Most people would argue that stocks which are heavily traded should have a fairly stable pricing pattern, but this is not so. And if this relationship does not hold for stocks then it should not hold for real estate or any other asset class.

During stock market corrections and other corrections of very widely held stocks, there have been instantaneous price drops of 10%, 20% or more. Consider GM's plunge from 35 to 28 overnight in mid-2005 or the massive plunge in the Dow Jones Industrial Average (Dow) in 1987 in two days! Very few people had to sell GM in 2005 or the Dow in 1987, and the efficient market theorists told us that assets were fairly valued, yet those assets each depreciated very rapidly. So why can't something similar happen in a local or even a national real estate market?

One needs only recall that in the late 1980's, the experts also said that home prices wouldn't collapse because people had to live somewhere.

What experience has shown over and over is that the experts are either lying and/or they are not as bright as they claim to be. The bottom line is to remember that the professionals have their interests closest to heart, and this clouds their vision and judgment, even if they might mean well.

Myth Number Eighteen:
A housing correction will not do much harm to the diversified US economy.

The greatest myth is that a housing correction will not harm the economy. There is currently close to $8 trillion in mortgage and home equity debt (versus relatively negligible margin debt in stock brokerage accounts). Since primarily the wealthy hold money in stocks, their spending patterns are not changed much when the stock market falls. On the contrary, with almost everyone in on the housing market these days, a correction would have a huge effect on spending. Studies have clearly shown that in recent decades, throughout the world, typical losses in real estate wealth have had devastating effects on consumer spending and economies. One needs only think of Japan's lost decade of the 1990's for confirmation of the effects of a large-scale housing correction.

These myths are in no way meant to be exhaustive. They only serve as an introduction to the rest of the book, where elements of these myths will be explored in greater depth, along with many areas not even touched upon to this point. As already explained, the myths are perpetuated by those who stand to gain from their perpetuation. They are intrinsically designed to become self-fulfilling prophesies.

Wall Street Acronym

I have been working for many years on cracking the secret Wall Street code, and I finally found the solution (this is in jest as there is no such official code).

W ait until most are in
A llow them to make some money
L et the air out of the balloon
L et them buy the dips

S ell them your stash
T ell them to sell
R e-enter the market
E ntice them to buy
E nhance the supply
T he cycle begins anew

2

FINANCIAL MARKET
FORCES

This section explores many of the forces involved in the financial markets, how those forces interact with each other, and ultimately how they affect the markets themselves. No investor should venture into the financial markets without at least a basic understanding of most of these pieces of the puzzle.

Bubble Theory

There are classic signs of a bubble, or a market top. All serious investors recognize them, or at least should be trained to recognize them, and ignore these signs at their own peril. It is in the interests of many advisors to keep this information from the small investor, and it is in the interests of many professionals and business people to suggest that the investor ignore the signs. Woe to the fool who follows their advice.

There is an easily recognizable pattern that has appeared throughout history which warns of a bubble. When it appears, many advisors will dismiss its existence, each time offering a litany of reasons for their dismissal. This pattern may take a hyperbolic- or exponential-like form and may describe the activity of an entire market, a market sector, an individual stock, real estate, art, oil or other commodities, or anything that is traded for financial gain.

Some of the most widely recognized bubble tops are those of the Dow Jones Industrial Average (Dow) of 1929, the Nikkei of 1990, the Nasdaq, Dow, and S&P500 of 2000, oil and gold in 1979/1980, and the 17th century Dutch tulip bulb mania. What an investor must learn is how to recognize a bubble, and then to get out of the market, or at least not to get in. The basic bubble pattern looks essentially the same when variables (usually asset price versus time) describing it are plotted on a sheet of paper or on a computer screen. Whether the pattern fits a hyperbolic or exponential-like curve is immaterial, because the curves are similar in appearance (please refer to the book cover for a typical bubble pattern). What they have in common is that the appreciating asset rarely goes straight up nor does it follow along a precise curve, but rather zigzags its way up between two defining curves. Such zigs and zags allow active traders to make money by buying and selling the asset at precise points along the way. When the curves which trace the highs and lows of the zigs and zags, respectively, finally come to a point, the peak of the asset bubble has been reached, and it's time to sell for good. Active traders will be tempted to trade the deflating bubble in a similar fashion to that which they traded it on the way up. Asset bubbles are natural phenomena, as they feed on the innate fear and greed of the human condition. They are the most important element in investing and at the same time are the easiest to recognize, provided one knows to look for them.

Savings

The 2005 personal savings rate in the US was its lowest since the Great Depression, having gone negative, down from a positive 8% of disposable income in 1990. This information suggests that US consumers have been conditioned to spend essentially all of their income, and they have become conditioned to treat their investments in their homes as their primary savings vehicles. Over the recent six-year period, consumers' average increase in personal consumption expenditures has been higher than their average increase in personal income. This is a very dangerous trend, because when (not if) housing prices correct, and possibly with that, the stock market, consumers will either have to drastically cut back consumption or go further into negative territory on aggregate personal savings. Either outcome will ultimately affect consumer spending, which will harm stock market performance as companies' revenues and profits decrease, and set in place a vicious downward cycle.

In the 1960's and 70's, the US personal savings rate was almost always at least a couple of percentage points above prevailing interest rates of the times, with interest rates peaking around the late 1970's/early 1980's. The US was a nation of savers. Since the mid-1990's, the savings rate has tended to be a couple of percentage points below prevailing interest rates. A close examination reveals that the dual effect of falling interest rates and savings rates through the 1980's and into the 90's helped propel the stock market upwards. The lower savings rates relative to interest rates of the late 1990's contributed to the last great surge upward in the stock market as consumers chose to spend their money on goods and services.

The savings rate has now gone essentially as low as it can go, so it is highly unlikely that a rising stock market can accompany rising interest rates from current levels. More likely, a sustained increase in savings rates will be necessary as interest rates rise, resulting in an accumulation of free cash which at some future time can be used, and ultimately allow the stock market to resume its gains. If the past provides a lesson, it is that a period of several years will be required in which savings rates exceed interest rates, so that the resulting savings can ultimately take the stock market higher.

Mutual Funds

The mutual fund industry has always tried to get investors into the market for the long haul, rather than letting them time the market, and for good reason. If the small investor's money is not in the market, then it is definitely not in a mutual fund company's funds, and it is therefore not generating any fee income. On the other hand, as long as money is invested in their funds, then mutual fund companies can count on a steady stream of management fees year after year. One of the techniques employed by mutual fund companies to convince investors not to attempt to time the market, and therefore, to keep money in mutual funds, has been to scare people. One of their greatest scare tactics has been to show potential investors the results of various studies revealing how little their returns would be if they had missed a particular number of days in the market (when the market rose significantly) over a certain period of time. Fund representatives might show the statistics as ten days over a one-year period, or perhaps, ten days over a ten-year period, or similar studies. The results would always show that if the investor had missed those best days, then his/her returns would be puny. I referenced this practice in myth number five in the earlier part of the book. I have never trusted these types of studies because I could see that these firms never presented the contrarian argument of having been out of the market on the ten worst performing days, which could support the concept of market timing. After all, it only makes sense that if the firms went to all the trouble to study one side of the argument that they would also analyze the other side. The investor should always beware when presented with only one side of a story.

A personal experience of mine can help illustrate what I refer to as "myth-building". A friend brought me to a seminar put on by a publicly traded network-marketing company. The company was starting up a new geographic division, so their management and sales team took a large room at a New York City hotel in the 1990's to recruit new sales representatives. My friend was attempting to recruit me for his "line". I had my guard up, but agreed to go. The show was business as usual as they brought one success story after another onto the stage, but never a story of failure. The ultimate was when one of their senior executives attempted to really sway the hundreds of potential recruits when he announced that we should not miss out on a golden opportunity, and that we should just think how happy we would have been had we bought shares in Microsoft in its early years. Up to that point I was actually beginning to think that maybe there was a possibility, but when he made the Microsoft statement, the gig was up. For me, it confirmed that this entire presentation was based on the absolute best case scenario, and that there would actually be very few winners. Of course he would be among the winners, as would the other top executives. My point is that mutual funds use a similar tactic when they tell you to just think if only you had your money with them on the ten best days, without mentioning the ten worst days.

Reputable organizations have reported that the effect of missing the worst days is essentially the mirror image of missing the best days. A monkey flipping a coin, therefore, has an equal chance of being in or out on these days and should pretty much perform in line with market averages over time, as long as that monkey obeys the advise given by the coin. On the other hand, a trained, experienced market timer should really be able to take advantage of these extreme days (in both directions) greater than 50% of the time, and therefore outperform the market average.

Until the early 1990's, investors put more money into funds with higher expense ratios and lower performance than into lower cost funds with higher performance. Why would investors do something like this?

Because of MARKETING!

A fund that charged higher fees tended to have more money for marketing. The additional marketing attracted additional funds from investors. The additional funds created more fees, and on and on it went. This is not dissimilar to what occurs with any company which engages in lots of marketing activity (drug companies created great wealth for their shareholders in the 1990's as they spent enormous sums of money on marketing activities).

Investors also are likely to have believed that higher fees would lead to higher performance through superior management. This thinking is rational to some extent, as many people perceive that the more something costs, the more value it has. But that has started to change. Now that low-cost funds and index funds in particular have gotten greater publicity and have a long-term track record, investors can make evaluations and reach conclusions that over the long term, a passive investor is highly likely to achieve superior performance by investing in low-cost (index) funds.

Mutual fund managers do not always have investors' best interests in mind. The easiest way for me to make my case is with an example. In late 2005, I attended a seminar put on by one of the best known mutual fund families, featuring one of its most successful mutual fund managers as its keynote speaker. I was already aware that there were lots of reasons for the stock market to go down, few for it to go up, that the real estate boom was over, that consumer spending as a percent of GDP had peaked at about two-thirds, that corporate profit margins were at all-time highs, and that ordinary income, capital gains, and dividend tax rates were at their lowest in nearly a century. I saw these things, along with soaring deficits, as negatives. He sited the rise in bankruptcies as a positive, signifying a market bottom. I disagree. His argument may hold in a normal market cycle, but this is not a normal market cycle. The US is under long-term fire, facing continued China/India economic threats combined with rising energy inflation issues, among many others. I believe these bankruptcies of the recent past are only the beginning of things to come. He suggested that another indication of a bottom is poor corporate image. But if recent poor corporate image is really a true indicator of a bottom, I ask why corporate executives were even more highly compensated in 2005 than ever, even after the stock market crash and all the scandals of recent years. These are just woefully inadequate means to determine market bottoms. So when he suggested that clients put their money into overseas developing markets, I winced. Market indexes showed many developing markets to be up 100% in the three prior years. Could it be he was sending his clients into investments which are about to undergo an intense correction as US consumers are forced to stop spending? Why didn't he just tell everyone to play it safe and put their money into conservative, high-yielding money market funds? Why didn't he tell us how he allocates his own money? I wanted to ask, but unfortunately he only had time for a few questions.

This manager clearly understands how the markets operate. He clearly understands that the US economy will slow down, and he must understand that when the US economy slows, there is a very high likelihood that all the emerging economies will follow, since they sell their goods to the US consumer. Yet he recommended that after an already strong run-up in the emerging markets that his clients put their money into those markets. The rationale made no sense to me. The only way I could justify his recommendation is that it is based on fee generation for the firm. Very small fees are generated in money market funds, and therefore, are not high on the radar of spokesmen for the firm. Perhaps he understood that the typical investor chases returns, and that he was better off steering that investor into one of his own family's funds rather than allowing that investor to go to the competition.

It is important to remember that very often a fund investor's worst enemy is himself. Numerous studies have been done over the years which show that the typical "surviving" ("surviving" because statistics for those which do not survive are generally thrown out, resulting in an upward bias in performance numbers) mutual fund has slightly underperformed the market index, and therefore achieved returns of perhaps 10% annually over several decades. This contrasts with closer to zero returns over the same period for mutual fund investors. The reason for this discrepancy is because the mutual fund investor tends to chase the best performing funds from prior years and ends up getting in near the top of a run, and then tends to sell the worst performing funds, getting out near the bottom.

Exchange-Traded Funds

I am a huge fan of exchange-traded funds (ETF's), and I was an early trader of them as well. They are safer than individual stocks, as they remove individual stock risk, and offer investors the ability to trade as much as they like. ETF's even have low expense ratios compared to actively managed mutual funds. But they can also create problems. As they get more and more popular, and all types of investors flock to them, there is the risk that prices of their component stocks could be driven up to levels which might otherwise not have occurred. Such a scenario is similar to what happened to stocks in major market indexes and index funds in the 1990's.

Professionals can take greater advantage of ETF's than can less knowledgeable investors, as the pros can time their trades, sell short, and/or buy and sell options with great skill. So, although the expense ratios are much lower than for actively managed mutual funds, small investors could take a much greater beating on total returns if they don't time their trades properly.

Total assets held in ETF's had gone from $1 billion in 1995 to $300 billion by 2005, and are still rising exponentially. Normally, classic bubble theory would suggest such a pattern to be a sign of eminent danger, but in this rare case it may also be seen as a sign of opportunity. The number of ETF's has also risen in a similar fashion, as their appeal is undeniable.

Closed-End Funds

People have been writing about closed-end funds for years, and letting the public know why they are not a good buy. They normally trade at a premium to their net asset values, meaning that they trade for more than they are worth. In other words, an investor can buy a similar index fund, mutual fund or ETF at fair market value, or at a discount to what he/she might pay for the closed-end fund. This is why many advisors suggest buying a closed-end fund only when it is selling at a discount to its net asset value, and maybe even not then, due to the numerous pitfalls of owning a closed-end fund.

One of these pitfalls is high dividend paying closed-end funds. Investors in such funds may not realize that often those funds are borrowing from one hand to give to the other. A fund may be paying a high dividend, but it could be taking the money from its own principal. This is similar to what occurs when a company with a declining stock price continues to pay a high dividend to its shareholders. As the company's worth deteriorates and the dividend remains steady, the yield actually increases. To the inexperienced, this seems like a great deal, and many educated and successful people buy into a high-yielding equity, solely on the basis of the dividend, which could easily be cut in the future. At any rate, when the fund pays out increasing dividends without increasing its real net worth, the Net Asset Value (NAV) of the fund may fall to cover the cost of these dividends. Many investors may not realize what's really happening, because as the fund's NAV falls, its shares may trade at a premium to its NAV. Some day when everyone realizes what is really going on at such a fund, its premium might drop precipitously, resulting in a large discount to NAV. When that occurs, an investor who would like to get out of the fund would have to sell at a large loss.

Hedge Funds

It looks like they're raking it in. I'll dub them the "billion dollar babies", because pretty soon these guys will all be worth a billion dollars each. And what great things have they done for society to earn this money?

Not much, really.

It was publicly disclosed in 2005 that more than a few handfuls of hedge fund managers earned over $200 million in 2003. Most of them were able to accomplish this by taking "2 +20", industry parlance for a 2% management fee and then another 20% of the fund's returns. To put this in perspective, let's assume an index fund manager is compensated in such a way. Assume that the fund has

$50 billion under management and assume that the fund's total return for the year is 15%. Under the management fee terms of 2 +20, the fund manager would take in $1 billion (2%) plus $1.5 billion (20% of the 15% annual return). In this hypothetical example, the manager would take in $2.5 billion in fees for a single year of managing this fund. Now scale down the numbers a bit and it's very easy to see how many hedge fund managers are making $200 million in a single year. And it's getting easier and easier to make this money. A hedge fund manager today can chose to emulate the S&P 500 by buying the SPY security, which is a low cost way to buy the index with a single trade, and then add a few individual positions to create a modification to the index in just a few more simple trades. Years ago when the 2 +20 fees took hold, at least it was a bit more cumbersome to build a portfolio. These days the process is easy, quick, and inexpensive. Just imagine if a company like Vanguard was charging 2 +20 instead of simply .09% (that's less than 1/20 of the 2% fee charged by the hedge funds). Assuming the market gives a few good years of double-digit returns, many of these hedge fund managers, who made $200 million in 2003, could make $1 billion in a few short years. At least up until now, people who made that kind of money had really built something useful to society. The craziest thing is that a monkey tossing a coin to select its investments can do just as well as nearly half of hedge fund managers.

These hedge fund cowboys have some deal. They have little to lose, and in many cases, they have little of their own money invested. To help make it easier to understand what's really going on in this industry, it's almost as if someone's rich uncle gave him $1 million, sent him to Las Vegas for a week, gave him more than enough money to cover his expenses, and told him that he could keep 20% of everything he made, but would have no penalty if he loses. The nephew might play conservatively initially, but as time was running out and he was just breaking even, chances are very good that he would start placing some very risky bets. After all, if he came back with the same $1 million he left with, chances are his uncle would send somebody else next time, or he would just put the money in the bank and earn 5% annually. If the nephew lost half of his uncle's million, his uncle might be angry at him, and possibly never speak to him again, but on the other hand, since the uncle still has so much money and he loves his nephew, he might just attribute the loss to bad luck and send his nephew on another trip. Assuming his nephew got lucky, and came back with a nice return, the uncle would let him keep 2% of the million and another 20% of the gains, minus his expenses. Got the picture? Welcome to the wonderful world of hedge funds. It is a business in which very ordinary people are literally making millions or tens of millions of dollars per year. Extraordinary people in the industry are making hundreds of millions or billions.

In recent years, the average hedge fund has performed slightly better than the market, as measured by the return on the S&P500, and for its essentially par performance (which may not even be based on real numbers, as the industry is not very opaque), its manager has been walking away with outrageous compensation of 2+20. To illustrate how ridiculous things can get, from the market top of the mid-1960's to the market bottom of the early 1980's, the stock market declined at a real average annual compound rate in the mid-to-high single-digits. Just imagine giving your hard-earned money to a hedge fund manager for a similar period (perhaps the next ten years), who achieves an annual net loss of 5% in real terms. Under such a scenario, he might outpace the market, yet you would still lose 5% per year in real terms. For this he would be paid 2% of your money, plus another 20% of his out-performance of the market, making your real loss even worse. Congratulations. You will have lost much of the purchasing power of your money while making your hedge fund manager a very wealthy person. Maybe you should think about putting your money into a safe, low-cost money-market fund for the next ten years, and cut the hedge fund manager off your welfare roles.

Hedge fund danger signs abound. Hedge fund fraud is on the rise. While it's well known that there are twice as many hedge funds (8000) with twice the money under management ($1 trillion) as there were in 2000, what's not as well known is the increasing number of incidents of foul play. The number of hedge fund fraud cases opened by the SEC has been climbing exponentially in recent years, albeit from a very low base, but it is important to keep in mind that the SEC generally only brings cases after there are public disclosures of problems. Taking into account that the SEC has little idea of what's going on at hedge funds, and that the funds have every incentive to hide losses and show gains, with no organization effectively policing them, and we have a recipe for disaster. I wonder how many cases of fraud will be brought once the stock (or bond) market has a large-scale move up or down, and many of the so-called "hedged" funds unravel. Industry observers will point out that hundreds of hedge funds go out of business every year. A great many of them close due to poor performance. This represents extraordinary turnover and hints of the potential instability in the industry.

Yet another problem with hedge funds is that many of them operate almost like private clubs, in which there may be many different types of agreements with different investor classes. Who knows how many hedge funds have secret arrangements which make an already non-opaque situation even less opaque. It all reminds me of the IPO market of the recent stock market bubble, when certain insiders had all sorts of privileges which were simply not given to the small investor. If I were invested in a hedge fund, I would demand to have a written statement informing me that the fund had no separate agreements with any investor class in the fund. If its managers refused to provide me with such a certified statement, I would demand my money back immediately.

Bubble theory applies to hedge fund analysis just as it does to all areas of investing and human behavior. Charting the growth of the number of hedge funds against time and connecting the points yields a curve tracing a classic bubble pattern, which represents one of the clearest signals to stay away from hedge funds. A similarly shaped curve presents itself in a graph showing the amount of net new money coming into hedge funds against time. The exponential nature of the curve tracing net new money from the late 1990's to present suggests that a peak has likely been reached.

I probably appear as though I am very negative on hedge funds. In general this is true, but I do recognize that there are some outstanding hedge funds out there. I also recognize that some hedge funds can and do have positive effects, as they are giving CEO's a taste of what I call "CEO-medicine". As hedge funds gain increasing power, they make greater demands of CEO's and give them shorter timeframes to achieve investor goals. Hedge funds potentially could also help force CEO compensation down to more realistic levels.

It should be noted that while I am in general very negative on hedge funds, I am not suggesting that mutual funds are the way to go. We could be in an investment environment in which overall financial market returns are in the low single-digits for many years to come. For an investor who is paying fees to a financial advisor in addition to fees for an actively managed fund, that investor's fees could eat up half of his/her total return. Such an arrangement could actually be even more expensive for that investor than investing in a hedge fund.

Funds of Funds

Schwab put together the first large-scale mutual fund supermarket in the 1990's which enabled investors to keep all their money under one roof and still be able to choose among best performing funds. Those investors were able to diversify while paying only moderate additional fees.

More recently, the hyper-growth of hedge funds has been accompanied by the hyper-growth of funds of hedge funds. This business enables a manager to take a fee for himself in exchange for putting together a collection of "well-managed" hedge funds for investors. Once this new manager's fee is added onto the 2 +20 of each individual hedge fund's fee within the fund of funds, there is nary a chance that the investor will come out ahead. Of course, though, he/she will have something to talk about at cocktail parties.

Just when I thought I had heard it all, I am starting to hear about people putting together funds of ETF's. It sounds like they may work in a way similar to mutual fund supermarkets, but we'll have to wait to see the final formats. But in these days of low cost trading when ETF's can all be held in any brokerage firm, there really is no need to put them all together into a supermarket, unless of course the purpose of doing so is to enrich the owner of the supermarket through various management and maintenance fees.

Power Players

It was reported in late 2005 that Ronald Perelman had won his lawsuit against Morgan Stanley for its role in his sale of Coleman to Sunbeam in 1998. The judgment is purported to be for over $1.4 billion. All this is for a seasoned CEO, who is certainly among the most sophisticated of investors. I have no problem with this judgment, as I believe perpetrators of misdeeds should be punished for their misdeeds, lest they will commit them again. Instead, where I see the irony is that this sum is approximately equal to the total sum of the settlement between all the Wall Street firms and Eliot Spitzer, on behalf of the small investors who were conned out of billions in the late 1990's and early 2000's. Worse is that only a few short years following the crash, those same firms are paying out about $20 billion in bonuses two years in a row! Eliot Spitzer went after Wall Street, but in the final analysis, doesn't it seem that he settled for too little, especially in light of what Perelman's attorneys were able to accomplish for him?

Wall Street Compensation

Bonus time has come and gone on Wall Street. It is a time when management takes stock of individual, group, division, and overall company profitability. Generally, roughly 50% of Wall Street income is paid out in compensation to its employees. The balance goes to cover other operating costs, with the leftovers going to shareholders. On Wall Street, when times are good, they are really good, and when times are bad, they are still really good. This is because when times are bad, Wall Streeters can rely on excellent compensation, and when times are good, everything extra is gravy. And when things are good, the gravy flows abundantly.

Wall Street tends to make its big money in different areas at different points in the economic and market cycles, and has come to rely on proprietary trading for an ever-increasing percentage of its profits in recent years, as volume and margins in other areas have fallen. Let's examine what goes on with proprietary trading on Wall Street. Proprietary traders are the people who are trading the firms' money (Hmmm, technically, they're trading the shareholders' money). This poses a risky situation for shareholders, though. Let's assume a firm's proprietary traders have a great year. In this case, they receive their already generous salaries, topped off by performance bonuses that can routinely be ten times their already generous salaries. Of course, some of this extra profit is retained by the firm (which can have the effect of driving the stock price higher) and/or paid out in dividends to shareholders.

But what happens if their traders bet wrong and lose lots of the firm's money? In this case, they still get their generous salaries. Maybe their bonuses are ONLY 100% of their salaries. Either way, shareholders take the loss as the value of the stock falls. This is one of the truly wonderful businesses in the world (if you can get the work), where the workers can lose lots of the firm's money, the shareholders suffer as the stock price falls, yet the traders and executives still keep their high paying jobs because somehow they have managed to convince the shareholders that nobody else can do their work. As if that's not enough, they then go on to convince the shareholders that they must continue being paid their generous salaries so that their firms can remain competitive with other firms (I guess if all the firms use this argument, all employees get raises).

Derivatives

The use of derivatives is exploding. Just about every financing method is now tied to derivatives. There is an alphabet soup of derivative products like mortgage-backed securities, asset-backed securities which can be tied to auto lending, credit card loans, music, or anything that can be repackaged and sold, and collateralized debt obligations, among many others. Credit-default swaps which did not exist ten years ago are now valued at over an estimated $8 trillion.

Derivatives may have reduced the risk of holding an individual asset, but this insurance has come at a cost. Nearly every asset purchased on credit today is in some form linked to a massive pool of derivatives which help reduce individual risk at the expense of greatly increasing systemic risk. By some estimates, neither the major Wall Street firms nor regulators can account for the holders of as much as half of the derivatives which have been repackaged and sold. It should be recalled that the banks make their money on transactions, so every time a bank repackages and sells a deal, it takes a fee. I wonder how many times bits and pieces of earlier deals are being repackaged and sold to other players for a new round of fees. I also wonder how many times these bits and pieces are repackaged and resold again, and how many of these bits and pieces ultimately end up in the very hands of the original creators of these products.

If you follow me, I am wondering if this is a great Ponzi scheme, in which "IOU's" are continuously packaged and repackaged, sold, and sold again, generating fees for the sellers on each sale, with no real benefits for society. It may turn out to be similar to the internet bubble, during which time many high-tech companies were simply selling each other their products, generating massive increases in revenues and profits, until it came time to collect the cash for those products. I don't think I have to tell anyone how that game ended, with reports of as much as 30% of purchased packaged software left unopened and sitting on shelves, and hundreds of companies completely unable to pay their debts. Funny how that word "packaged" keeps appearing.

International Markets

There are numerous issues to consider when venturing into foreign investment markets. I am going to focus on a few of those areas in the hopes of steering the small investor away from potential disaster. Many investors have observed the Korean market move up 300% from 1998 to present, and they want in at any cost. But a quick look at any graph tracing the path of the Korean market (omitting echo bubbles of 1999 and 2001), reveals a classic bubble theory top occurring in 2006. It is highly unlikely that upward moves can be sustained from this point without a significant market correction. An investor's broker or financial advisor will probably never tell the investor this, because either he doesn't understand it or because he wants to get the investor to invest more so that he can have long-term money under management from which he can collect fees.

I was on the floor of the Korean Stock Exchange in the summer of 1988 (two weeks prior to their Olympics), just as that bubble was popping, and since that time I have witnessed the Korean market go through several major moves up and down. I don't mean to single out the Korean market, but it is a good proxy for all the emerging markets, as they have all gone through similar cycles at similar points in time. What the reader should take away from this discussion is that when everyone is rushing to these markets, a careful investor should be walking away from them.

Investors need to be particularly careful when investing in emerging markets because each behaves under its own set of rules. For example, with China growing at 9% per year, it is very tempting to invest in its stock market. But for some reason, its stock market has remained essentially flat in recent years. How can this be? Why are other emerging markets' stock markets moving higher so rapidly when they are experiencing lower economic growth rates and have smaller populations and economies than does China? Many variables can contribute to stock market moves. Among them, emerging markets tend to have relatively small total market capitalizations and can therefore be moved up or down by large speculators, including their own governments. As a general rule, therefore, it is best to buy low and sell high, with the economic cycle. It must always be kept in mind that if the Nasdaq can fall by 80% in less than a 3-year period, it can happen anywhere and anytime.

It is very important to understand the concept of correlation when investing in international markets. Advisors have long suggested diversification of an investment portfolio as a safety measure, incorporating a correlation factor to designate how well investments are diversified. A figure of 1.0 denotes perfect correlation, and a figure of zero denotes no correlation whatsoever. Correlation between the US and the rest of the world was much closer to zero than to one in the 1980 timeframe. A lot has changed since then, as the correlation is far closer to one now than it is to zero. Many advisors continue to argue that investors can diversify by putting their money overseas, but that is not really true anymore, as the economies and stock markets of the world have become much more codependent. Unfortunately for small investors, the truth is probably that their advisors are so used to disseminating this diversification strategy that they are still using the same old argument even though everything has changed. Government practices bear out my argument, as central banks appear to be working along the same lines, continuing to link trade and interests rates. This would imply that movements in stock markets will become more of a family affair than in the past, and for the time being all will tend to move up and down together. This would imply that one is better off diversifying their investments in some other way, or at least seeking countries with correlations of far less than 0.5 with the US, provided they exist.

On Perpetuation of Myths

When I was an engineer with General Electric Aircraft Engines during the "cold war", I volunteered for an assignment on one of the US air force bases, where I worked hands-on with the enlisted men and women. I always respected those who enlisted in the military, and did so even more after witnessing how diligently these men and women worked with the goal of protecting each other and the rest of us. I have always had a heavy heart when I hear of bad news befalling our servicepeople. In honor of them (I believe every American should know these statistics), I include an exercise to help illustrate a point.

Ask around to see who knows the number of servicepeople the US lost in WWII. The number is somewhere between 500,000 and 600,000. Then ask how many were lost on Omaha beach on D-Day. The answer is around 3000, or roughly the same as the number of people lost on "9/11". Most people will think the number lost on D-Day was far greater than 3000. Also ask how many were lost at Pearl Harbor. The answer is about 2500, with one-half being on a single ship which was sunk. Again most will believe the total number to be far higher. Finally, ask what percent of the current US population has at one time in their lives served in the US military. Again the answer will surprise, only this time to the upside. Approximately ten percent of the US population has served! Memories and knowledge of these important events and figures are easily shifted in our minds, proving that reality and perception (and conditioning) are often far apart.

We collectively imagine numbers and valuations to be much higher or lower than they should be. This is what happens during stock market and real estate market bubbles. We all get so involved emotionally, that we forget reality. Hopes and emotions take over, and truth and fact take a back seat, and perhaps even all but disappear. Something similar even happens in human relationships.

Take the much discussed "love at first sight" as an example. Those who are taken by an initial image want to believe that everything else flows into place, so they convince themselves that there are few or even no flaws. No matter that their friends and family point out flaws, because the smitten simply does not see the flaws, or refuses to see them. This too is what happens near a market top when the few bears are trying to make everyone see the flaws of the market or the stock, or other asset. But the collective community of investors (being smitten) refuses to see the top or creates reasons why the bears are wrong. In the end, the bears are proven right and the bubble pops, just as the victim of love at first sight always finds out that there are flaws.

Myths have always been a part of the human condition, and they will likely never disappear. In some ways they are necessary. The successful investor must understand that myths are here to stay, and that they will always be present in the investment markets. The investor must then learn how to read the sign-posts and to act before everybody else does.

Google

This is the story of Google. Google was created in 1998 as a search engine employing an evolutionary (not revolutionary) internet search technique. Google experienced outstanding revenue and profitability growth. By 2004, its founders and venture investors thought it was a good time for an IPO. Many investment banks came out negative on Google leading up to the IPO, yet after going public, the stock managed to quadruple by late 2005. How could the stock make such a move when Wall Street said it was overvalued at the time of the IPO? Why would the firms say such a thing? And if they couldn't get this right, why should we believe anything they tell us? These are great questions! And the answer to the last question is that we should believe very little of what the firms and their analysts tell us. We have to read between the lines when they express their views.

Google's founders wisely decided that they wanted their IPO to be as democratic as possible for a number of reasons. Wall Street firms love IPO's, as they are a source of big, fast, easy money. Wall Street firms typically get 7% of the total offering in fees, and often get a number of shares for themselves. Further, by being able to provide their best clients with shares of hot IPO's, and keeping themselves at the top of the league tallies, they virtually guarantee themselves more business and profits in the future. Google's management wanted to keep its offering expenses as low as possible and get its shares into as many investors' hands as possible. The Google boys probably understood that by getting the stock into lots of hands, they could count on those new stockholders to remain or become valuable customers. They did this by using a Dutch Auction IPO method offered by Hambrecht & Company. Many of the larger banks on Wall Street and their big clients were angered by this deal, and decided to punish Google for its brazenness, and to send a message to all future offenders that they too will suffer the consequences should they try to follow in Google's footsteps.

To their dismay, all the Wall Street firms succeeded in doing was lowering Google's offering price somewhat, and we all know what happened since. Those who refused to listen to the powerful, angry Wall Street firms did quite well for themselves, and those who did listen were forced to buy in at much higher prices later. This is the story of Google.

Speculators

There are all types of speculators. Every investor must be aware that they exist and that at any time they can turn a market trend upside down. Some speculators look for major news events in order to take control of an entire industry. We saw this in 1999 and into 2000 in internet stocks, as well as in the stock market in general. Now we are seeing it in the price of oil. The true drivers of price are not necessarily tied to only supply and demand, but are also in the hands of powerful hedge funds and other speculators which dominate the markets. When they sensed that interest rates would stay low for an extended period and put the world economy into hyper-growth, speculators did what came natural to them. They began driving up the price of oil and gold. Estimates vary, but many believe that up to one-third of the price of oil is due to speculators. These same speculators do not simply buy and hold. Many of them trade as they push the trendline higher and higher. This enables them to pocket trading gains several times during a multi-year move.

Speculators and arbitrageurs were also able to take full advantage of the carry trade, in which they borrow money from markets with extremely low interest rates and reinvest that money in markets with significantly higher interest rates. Over the years, the world has even witnessed the ability of speculators to move entire stock markets of certain emerging market economies, so an investor must never underestimate the power of some of the larger ones.

General Motors

Every stock has a story to tell. General Motors (GM) has gotten a lot of attention lately, and for good reason. Just about everyone has an interest in it. Both labor and management have a keen interest, as the unfolding story at GM could serve as a guide for all future labor negotiations. Its stock and bonds are among the most widely held. It's one of the few Dow stocks in history that could potentially go from being a Dow stock straight into bankruptcy. Should GM go into bankruptcy, reverberations would be felt throughout the entire automobile industry, and throughout other industries as well.

Recent surveys have been suggesting that the vast majority of consumers would not buy a car from a company in bankruptcy, which could make it very difficult for GM or any other auto manufacturer to emerge from bankruptcy once filed. Further, should GM go the bankruptcy route, Ford would likely be forced to follow suit, as it could no longer compete with the more competitive cost structure of an emergent GM. A double filing would have the effect of driving the stock prices of all the other auto manufacturers down, as they would no longer enjoy the immense cost advantages they had been accustomed to having.

The US government would certainly not prefer a bankruptcy filing, as this would mean the tax system would have to rescue the pension and health care plans for GM and Ford retirees. Further, GM and Ford have become major users of high-tech equipment and services, and their filing for bankruptcies could be a major blow to the US high-tech industry in addition to their more traditional suppliers. Their bankruptcies would cause irreparable harm to the US economy and potentially have ripple effects throughout the rest of the world.

It is clear to me that there are so many forces working to keep GM alive and out of bankruptcy, that it is highly likely to be averted. If this is obvious to me, then why do so many analysts claim GM will be in bankruptcy within a couple of years? The answer may be that these analysts either don't know what they are doing, or they may be attempting to game the market. In the latter case, they may be attempting to force down the stock price of GM. When the price is driven down considerably, they can then change their calls to "buys", and their followers can step in and buy the stock. As more believers and aggressive traders get on board and buy the stock, the price could rise considerably. It may then be time to cash out of the position and start the process all over again, driving the stock price down. This pattern can and does repeat itself over and over as is evidenced by the price chart of GM's stock. Is there any other way to explain fluctuations of 30% several times a year when everyone pretty much could guess what was going to happen with management, labor, and investors?

Even the Bush administration cares more than they let on. Just imagine if the administration came out and said that there would be a bailout or that they would never let GM fail. Then labor and management would have no incentive to make the large-scale changes needed, and a bailout would become a self-fulfilled prophesy, encouraging the current no-win situation to go on indefinitely. Only by stating that there will be no bailout is there a chance that a rescue won't be necessary. In the end, of course, the administration understands what could happen to the economy in the event of a bankruptcy filing by GM, and there is only a very slim chance they would allow it to occur.

The point of this exercise is to illustrate some primary forces acting on a particular company's stock price, and to show how easily that price can be moved. At the same time, provided an investor understands how all these forces interact, this stock can be a beautiful thing to trade.

Market Sectors

The fortunes of entire industries can change in a few short months. Witness the technology industry following the year 2000 (Y2K) bubble. Technology is down to about 15% of S&P500 stock market capitalization in 2006 from its peak of over 30% in 2000. Is it a good time to be in tech now? Maybe it is and maybe it isn't.

Medium-term supply, medium-term demand, and percent makeup of total market capitalization are among the variables that determine major market moves of different sectors of the stock market. The reason I focus on the medium term is because the short term is too short to have market moving consequences of any sustainability. Sure, we might get a one day, one week or one month move, but that will be all there is to account for a short-term change, and all the big money will likely have gotten there first. And a long-term issue will result in a more gradual change in stock price or industry valuation.

It is the medium-term scenario which offers the opportunity to make a lot of money on a sector or on the individual securities within that sector. Take the technology bubble of the 1990's. Its two major drivers were both seen as medium-term phenomena. The Y2K problem was approaching, and everything was being replaced or fixed in preparation. This was going on for much of the 1990's. The Y2K issue, along with the race to build out the internet, was anticipated to drive spending for several years. Taken together, the wise among us could see we were in for a medium-term bull-run in technology, and in fact, the tech sector peaked in 2000 at over 30% of S&P500 market capitalization.

Energy, which is currently at about 10%, was approximately 5% of S&P market capitalization only a few short years ago. Again, the reason has been due to medium-term prospects. The markets were coming off ridiculously low prices for oil, and interest rates were low, spurring ferocious world-wide growth, and with that, ferocious world-wide demand. Long term, the assumption is that the energy problem will be dealt with either by new oil discoveries, new energy alternatives, new oil extraction techniques, and/or slowing oil demand. A short-term spike would not create a good investment opportunity, as any gains would soon be surrendered. In the case of energy, as in the case of technology, the market needed to see (and receive) conditions which could create a multi-year surge in demand beyond immediate supply. Such conditions give sustained sector moves.

What could be the next mover? One could argue that as interest rates move up, financials should no longer account for 20% of market capitalization. A good argument could be made that this could be cut in half to perhaps 10%. Another area to consider might be the 13% accounted for by healthcare. Healthcare's share of GDP is about 14%, so this number is pretty much in line, but healthcare is growing rapidly. Within this figure may be the real opportunity. Drug companies are down to about 6% of market capitalization from more than double that a few years ago. With the fear of avian flu and the possibility of a few blockbusters on the horizon for an assortment of ailments and conditions, everything can change very rapidly. Besides, what is more important than paying to stay alive and well? Of course, prior to making an investment decision on the drug companies, one must consider the rise of the biotechnology companies and how that may affect the future of traditional drug companies. One could also reason that since no hard goods can be made without materials, the materials sector should be more highly valued.

Sectors are also affected by the interest rate cycle. As the Fed raises and lowers interest rates to cool and stimulate the economy, respectively, sectors respond differently. I choose not to focus on this aspect of sector analysis in this book because all the pros play this game, and because so much attention has already been given to which sectors are supposed to go in and out of favor at various points in the interest rate cycle. I recommend reading up on the trends in one of the many publications that have been written concerning this subject and incorporating that information into a general trading and investing strategy.

What should be taken away from this section is that market sectors have always moved up and down in their own cycles which can either be dependent on or independent of the overall market. The investor's goal is to attempt to identify which sectors are setting up for possible sustained moves, and to get there before the competition does.

Market Timing

The pros are always telling the small investor not to time the market. So why then are so many of them fixated on doing it themselves?

There are best times of the day, best days of the week, best days of the month, best holidays, best seasons, best quarters, best years, best years in various types of cycles, and naturally along with all the rules for best times to buy, there are best times to sell (and these are only the basics). One thing notably absent from this list is best and worst months. The Dow (Dow Jones Industrial Average) was down on average over the last century in only three months of the year, with only one of those months being down significantly. September's average decline was about 1%. But September is also the only month when the market has fallen more times than it has risen, so following a summer rally it may be a very good idea to be out of the market when September comes around. Every professional who invests in the market knows these statistics very well, and this is why many seasoned investors are very wary coming into September. October has the dubious distinction of being the month of great crashes (think October, 1987, and 1929, among others). A great deal of professional hedging and market timing goes on during this period to take advantage of market volatility. Long-term studies have also shown that the vast majority of market gains have occurred between November and May, hence the old Wall Street saying; "sell in May and go away".

As for quarterly returns, another strong trend emerges. Returns for the Dow over the last century show the fourth quarter of the year to handily beat the other quarters. Generally this out-performance occurs following the September and/or October dip. In the last ten years, average fourth-quarter returns have been in the high single-digits. Even in the years 2001 and 2002, when the US stock markets were in severe correction mode, they still managed to give returns of at least 10% in the final quarter of each year. These outsized returns may have come in reaction to the negative returns through the first three quarters of each of those years. Perhaps the collective hope of market participants at the traditionally strong time of the year is what drove the market to yield such impressive quarterly returns, or perhaps it was that combined with other market forces. With so many money managers and professionals being paid based on market performance for the year, all these participants could effectively "will" the market up in the final quarter, so that they wouldn't fall too far short of their goals. Either way, it is clear that there has been a trend in place for a long time, and that trend got much stronger in recent years, especially down years. Much of what strengthened this trend is the concentration of so much money in a few powerful hands, and of course as word gets out, and more investors become aware of these trends, a breaking point will be reached. At that breaking point, the power players will shift gears, and the magnitude of this recent trend will fall, only to re-emerge somewhere else.

This pattern of human behavior is not unlike what goes on at a popular restaurant, nightclub, or with a trendy clothing line. Once word gets out and everyone is trying to get on board, the movers and shakers are off to a new locale or style. And they often move together to drive the new trend.

These are just a few examples of the information which is available to all investors. The numbers have been shown to be statistically significant by their mere existence over such a lengthy period, so I am stunned to still hear from pundits that the markets cannot be timed. I will go into more depth on timing the markets and trading in another book, but for now the small investor should never believe anyone who tells him that the market cannot be timed. It's almost akin to being told that the earth is flat, and because the "authorities" or the experts said so, then it must be true.

Hedging Bets

It is in the interests of Wall Street firms to try to get the investor to buy as many types of products as they can sell. Why?

Because they can!

Wall Street firms' primary goals are to make money, and one of the ways they do this is by charging fees. So when an investor expresses nervousness about an investment, that investor has opened himself up to a whole new area of fee income for the firms. This area involves "buy" options, "call" options, shorts, spreads, and all other sorts of more exotic techniques. Before getting involved in these areas, the investor must understand that in addition to paying additional fees for employing these techniques, that in the long term he will not be able to outperform the professionals, and will therefore come out on the losing end. The fact that these products are more complicated to understand than simply buying and selling stocks puts the investor at an even greater disadvantage than normally, as the pros will again turn to their heavy firepower to outmaneuver the investor in every way. In addition, countless hours will be consumed while attempting to understand it all (and let's face it … time is money). The investor must always remember that Wall Street is in the business of making money, just as the casinos are in the business of making money, and they will not introduce a product that will cause them to come out on the losing end. Given that the business is a zero-sum game, the small investor will lose.

I hedge my bets by purchasing what I call "stock market insurance", and here is how it works. I might believe the market will go down, but I don't want to totally miss the upside in the event I am wrong. So I buy a few high quality names that have gone down or been flat for a while. This way I don't completely miss a move up, but lose very little if I am correct and there is a large downside move. The reason this works is that it is similar to purchasing insurance for anything else in life. A typical person probably rarely makes a claim, yet pays each year for health insurance, homeowners insurance, auto insurance, disability insurance, travel insurance, umbrella policies, and even pet health insurance. A business owner also pays for workers compensation insurance, professional and general liability insurance, and a host of other insurances. A typical person can spend tens of thousands of dollars per year on insurance and may hardly even use it. And it's all for the small chance that it may be needed. I equate the purchase of insurance to cover other aspects of my life with purchasing the stocks of a few high quality names even if I believe there is a high likelihood the market will move down. This way, if I am wrong, at least I get to participate to some extent in the upward move. If I am correct and the market moves down, then I have sacrificed a very small percentage of my portfolio, and will be able to buy a lot more at much lower prices in the future. It's really a win-win situation, and one that should show that an investor really does not need to get involved with all of Wall Street's complicated hedging techniques, which in the end, only serve to enrich the professionals.

Games with Interest Rates

It was 2003 and I still had a lot of my money with Harris Direct, the offspring of DLJ Direct and CSFB Direct. I was earning extremely low interest rates in their money-market fund while waiting for some good IPO's to make up for all the disasters they had so readily handed to me during the prior few years. I conned myself into believing that if I showed loyalty to them, that I would somehow be rewarded. Unfortunately for me, the IPO market had dried up, so even if I had a chance of getting a good IPO from them to make up for past events, it became increasingly obvious that there wasn't going to be one. At that moment I vowed that going forward I would be very watchful of interest rates in addition to everything else. You see, interest rates are one of Wall Street's dirtiest little tricks, and I had taken my eye off the ball during the bubble meltdown.

Shift forward to early 2005 when I opened my mail and found that my bank account interest rate had dropped from 2% to ½% overnight. I guess one of the special short-term promotions had run its course. In this situation, the bank is counting on me being unable to perform the calculation to determine the interest rate, or if the interest rate is stated somewhere, it is likely hoping I will not bother to observe the new, much lower rate. If the bank (or brokerage firm) can pass this through to just 25% of their customers for a few months before those customers catch on, the bank will have boosted its earnings that quarter significantly (at their clients' expense).

Many people are accepting far lower rates than they could receive, and all it takes to prevent this from occurring is a little vigilance. Readers might be wondering why it is so easy for the banks to get customers to accept lower interest rates than they should. One big reason is psychological. People were used to receiving virtually no interest in 2002 and 2003, and had acquired a mindset that money in interest-bearing accounts does not actually earn anything significant at all. With such a mindset, it is understandable that people would devote little time to monitoring the rapidly increasing risk-free interest rates that were suddenly available to them. Another reason is that people can be a bit lazy, and might not believe that the monitoring of interest rates is worth their time. But it is worth their time, and it's worth their time no matter how much or how little money they have. This is so, because a person's net worth and cash position are a reflection of how much money that person's time is worth, and no matter where that person falls on this scale, the interest rate he earns on his money should have the same relative worth to him. But the biggest reason of all for accepting low rates may be because people don't even know where to go for information on interest rates. I go to imoneynet.com on the internet for my weekly update of yields at many of the largest money-market funds so I can stay on top of things. Interest rates vary within banks and brokerage firms, and often the customer needs only to request the higher rate to get it.

The lesson here is that banks and brokerages use interest rates to their advantage because they can. There is no requirement that they go out of their way to make sure the investor is getting the highest rate available. In this sense, it's no different than shopping for a new car or a computer, or anything else. Prices vary, and it's up to the consumer to shop around for the best deal. In the case of interest rates, however, the shopping never ends, because the terms can change on a daily basis.

Corporate Profits

Corporate profits as a percentage of GDP hit a four-decade high of about 11% in 2005. This is near the same level of the peak at the end of the 1950's/1960's bull run. Profits have come from a low of approximately 6% in the early 80's (not surprisingly when the great bull market began), which is really a much more reasonable number in a free and competitive marketplace. What frightens me is that profitability is coming off a very high number amidst the negative personal savings in this country. I wonder what might happen when the consumer, who accounts for approximately two-thirds of spending, finally balks at paying up.

What if the figure falls below the 6% level on the way down? At first thought, this sounds great for the consumer, but it would clearly have a devastating effect on stock prices and possibly on the economy, which in turn could be catastrophic for the consumer.

Debt Explosion

Everyone has been questioning whether the American consumer has taken on too much debt. About 25% of mortgage debt is adjustable. As interest rates rise and adjustable rates reset, consumers will find themselves with significant increases in their monthly debt payments on their mortgages, home-equity loans, and credit cards. Further consider that interest-only mortgages were virtually non-existent only a few short years ago, and by 2005, they accounted for about 25% of mortgages. Interest-only mortgages were previously utilized by sophisticated investors and home buyers who could benefit from the tax advantages offered by such mortgages. Recently, these mortgages have been used primarily by lower income, less sophisticated buyers, who may not even be benefiting from their tax advantaged attributes. These instruments have recently become increasingly utilized to bend traditional lending rules (which served as a safety net) to get more people into homes which they could otherwise not afford. Sadly, the government regulatory bodies have been asleep at the wheel, much in the way they were asleep prior to the recent stock market crash.

According to the Fed, revolving debt has increased six-fold in the last 2 decades to about $750 billion. A great deal of this increase can be attributed to the combination of low interest rates and very lenient credit extension to consumers. Unfortunately, such situations rarely end with pleasantries. Recall the easy credit in the form of margin debt to purchase stocks in the late 1920's. Recall the problems with the extended real estate market in the late 1980's, and the ensuing savings and loan fiasco. Well, one doesn't need to be a rocket scientist to know that when the music stops playing this time around, there will be lots of people who can't find their chairs.

Tapped Out

There is increasing evidence that the consumer is tapped out from rising energy and health care costs, and an uncontrollable urge to spend at retailers. Evidence suggests that credit card accounts past due and home equity loan delinquencies are on the rise, and delinquency rates are shooting up for nearly all types of consumer loans. Things are getting worse, and as interest rates rise, they will keep getting worse. Tougher bankruptcy laws enacted in 2005 will force consumers to tighten up on their spending even more than they otherwise might have.

Consumer Sentiment

By November, 2005, the University of Michigan consumer sentiment figure for October had reached a 13-year low of 74. Many optimists attribute this decline to the hurricanes, rising energy prices and the Iraq situation, and site the subsequent bounce back in consumer confidence as evidence that the worst is behind the country. Do not be tempted by these optimists, because the US is in the first-half of a 30-year hurricane cycle, and can be pretty sure the hurricanes will be back again next summer, the summer after that, and the following summers as well. Energy prices will remain high, and the Iraq situation is likely to linger for quite some time. Add higher interest rates, the debt explosion, the twin-deficits, and the Iran situation to this mix, and all the necessary ingredients are in place for considerable market corrections.

Creditor Nation No More

In the early 1980's, the US was a creditor nation to the tune of a fraction of a trillion dollars. I can remember an article I hung on my family's refrigerator in the late 1970's (I was in high school) which was about all the money the US was lending to the rest of the world. The crazy thing is that now the US is encroaching on a level of debt to the rest of the world of about $3 trillion (and is still lending and gifting money to "needier" nations). This, along with the negative high-tech trade balance do not portend for good things. To halt the falling dollar, interest rates will have to rise, putting the world economy at risk of a slowdown.

But even worse, does the US really wish to be "owned" by other countries? Make no mistake about it. This is what debt is. When others lend you money, it is no different than owning you. People with large amounts of debt are slaves to their masters, and their masters are the banks and mortgage lenders, whose own masters may turn out to be China. Do we really wish to some day be fully accountable to China?

The percent of US Treasury debt owned by foreigners seems to be following a classic bubble pattern which I so often see these days. It has soared from about 5% in 1970 to 55% in 2005! Bubble theory suggests to me that the figure could frightfully go to 80% or even 90% before undergoing a significant correction, but hopefully the growing awareness of this problem will stop it in its tracks before it gets to that level. As this number increases, however, the US loses more and more control of its own destiny, and that makes its financial markets very vulnerable to outsiders for the first time since the US emerged as the leader of the free world in the last century.

The Vicious Cycle of Interest Rates

"I'm caught in a trap, I can't get out ..." were the words uttered by the great one, Elvis Presley. Only this time instead of the love Elvis sang about, the US consumer should be singing about low interest rates. After all, who doesn't love low interest rates? Anyone who borrows money loves them, whether those interest rates are in the form of low credit card rates or low mortgage interest rates.

But there are people who don't love low interests rates or the debt which follows. Who are these people? One group of people is those who don't like debt. They remember from experience or learned from history what debt can do to people and economies. Another group is those who live on fixed income. They include the increasing numbers of the retired with little or no savings, whose income is determined by interest rates paid on their savings accounts or by inflation-indexed Social Security payments. They might also include the poor and the disabled, who are also dependent on payments determined by prevailing interest rates. Another growing group is businesspeople who are fearful that their customers are too leveraged thanks to the low rates, and that at some point, defaults will start rising rapidly, having a bad effect on the entire economy. Yet another group is those who are wary of the financial markets in general, and prefer to keep their money in safe, interest-bearing investments. A final group is those who would like to buy a home, but recognize that low interest rates have driven home prices up to unaffordable and unsustainable levels.

The vicious cycle of low interest rates tends to beget lower interest rates (until it stops working). When the Fed lowers interest rates, rates fall at all the lending institutions. This gives consumers more of an incentive to borrow and spend, and more of a disincentive to save (lower bank yields and money-market fund yields). The net effect is consumers borrow more, spend more, invest more, and save less. This cycle props up the returns of all types of businesses, which see their stock prices rise, and the stakeholders (shareholders and employees) of those businesses begin to spend more themselves. The increasing spending by consumers and businesses continue to drive up the values of real estate and financial assets, while savings rates fall. The cycle repeats itself over and over until something new happens ... INFLATION. That is the point where the Fed gets fearful and begins raising rates to slow things down. Usually this would be enough to put an end to the asset bubbles, but as we know from prior experience, asset bubbles have minds of their own. They are alive. They feed on themselves. They feed on greed. They feed on hope. They feed on fear (fear of being left behind). They feed on myths. And then, suddenly, they pop!

Real Federal Funds Rate

In the early 1970's, the real fed funds rate (that is the fed funds rate, adjusted for inflation) plunged from about 7% to approximately negative 4% in about a year. It then fluctuated rapidly between 12% and zero over the next few years. In more recent history it also experienced great fluctuation. In 1991 it was at zero, by 2000, at 5%, and for the last few years, essentially at zero (I actually feel that we have been well into negative territory due to my strong belief that the reported inflation numbers are managed in order to keep real interest rates down). The US economy is now coming off a recent multi-year period in which one month the Fed claimed to be worried about deflation, and the next it was worried about inflation. Either scenario is no good for the markets because each affects the behavior of consumers and businesses, and the stability of economies and governments.

The mood of the market and of market participants can swing abruptly (aren't we all a bit bipolar when it comes to money and investments?) as fears of deflation or inflation take hold. This should be telling everybody a few things. First, the Fed must respond to strong and erratic market forces on occasion, and it must do so rapidly. These responses can change the direction of sentiment from fears of inflation to fears of deflation, or vice versa, and obviously have consequences on economies and on financial markets. Second, rates (and markets) can be viewed over the relative short term (1 to 2 years) and/or over the relative long term (20 to 50 years). The recent past reveals a down trend in rates which occurred from 1980 to 2004, accompanied by rapid fluctuations within that down trend. Such fluctuations give investors the opportunity to make money by trading, whereas the longer-term down trend gives the opportunity to make money through buying and holding quality investments. Third, there is a real danger that the long-term trend has reversed, and that interest rates have begun a climb that could last for 20 to 50 years in a worst case scenario. Such an environment would be a very bad one for a buy and hold investment strategy (which is exactly what most people have been conditioned to do). In other words, be very careful. This means buying and holding quality when rates are trending down, and either trading quality names or sitting in solid short-term securities (short-term Treasuries or money-market funds) when rates are fluctuating or trending up.

Where Are Interest Rates Going?

Interest rates are steadily moving up in a channel, and according to the technical, fundamental, and economic analysis I practice, this trend should remain in place until the lower trend line is broken to the down side. So despite the talk around town, do not expect a let up in Fed increases until there is a clear change in trend.

Stock Market, Interest Rates and Inflation

The trend of the stock market tends to follow the trend in interest rates. When interest rates go up, stocks tend to go down, and when interest rates go down, stocks tend to go up. And, of course, interest rates follow inflation. There are two types of inflation figures compiled by the government, core CPI inflation and CPI inflation. The core CPI excludes food and energy prices because they can undergo great short-term fluctuations. Recently, however, the CPI has surged ahead of the core CPI, and with an extreme drop in the price of oil nowhere in sight, the core CPI will itself rise rapidly to catch up to the CPI.

How do I know this?

If we go back to the last times the CPI surged ahead of the core CPI to such an extent (which was on two occasions in the 1970's), the core CPI followed with no more than a one-year lag. Even without historical data, this should be obvious to anyone who spends time thinking about the relationship between the two measurements of CPI. If both variables measure inflation, with one factoring in all the short-term fluctuations and the other smoothing all those fluctuations, it makes perfect sense that if the short-term fluctuations do not correct themselves within a certain timeframe, the forces which generate those short-term fluctuations will work their way into the smoothed CPI (the core CPI). What must happen in such a scenario is that one of these inflation measuring variables must fall, or one must rise, or they must meet somewhere in the middle. Since I see this and you see this, the Fed must also see it, which means Ben Bernanke (Bernanke) will continue raising rates until he is satisfied that the increases in CPI turn into decreases in CPI, resulting in a leveling off in the rate of increase in core CPI.

Real Inflation

Economists have been using terms like real rates of return and real interest rates for decades to account for the effect of inflation on returns. I would like to introduce a term called "real inflation" which adjusts the "stated" inflation rate by an appropriate factor to arrive at a "true" inflation rate. I believe that real inflation should be based on the cost of goods and services that a reasonable person needs to purchase. In my model, such goods and services consist of food and clothing essentials, shelter, necessary home maintenance, transportation, energy, tax preparation, basic communication services, health care, and education.

Over the past few years (2003 to 2006), the cost of a median home in the US is up over 10% per year (and since nearly 70% of households own a home, cost of owning should be used rather than cost of renting), typical energy costs are up over 10% per year, food is up about 3% per year (although many restaurants have been raising prices at much higher rates), clothing is essentially unchanged, the cost of an automobile is also essentially unchanged, but the cost of maintaining a vehicle is certainly up, as is the cost of public transportation (just hail a cab or ride the Metro in New York City). Home maintenance is up about 5% per year (give your plumber a call tonight and be sure to check your cable TV bill), tax preparation services are up about 8% per year (your accountant), health insurance and related costs are up about 10% per year (my health insurance costs, and probably yours as well), and school tuition is up about 7% per year. There is no end in sight to some of these rates of increases, like health care, which for many people costs as much or more than their cost of shelter. Yet the health care component in the inflation index is hardly accounted for when compared to the housing component. Oddly, college tuition, which impacts all families on average, is virtually unaccounted for in the government's calculation of inflation.

In its calculations, the government further brings down the inflation rate by showing that consumers get more bang for the buck from technology (i.e. computers are more powerful and cost less, so this has the effect of being deflationary), but perhaps too much weighting is being given to things like computers and iPods. After all, how important are these things in our lives? Isn't it far more important to have basic food, shelter and clothing, and to have proper health care, and hasn't it become a necessity to send our children to proper schools for a decent education (including college) to make sure they don't end up as paupers? These are the true essentials, and therefore these are the costs on which inflation should be based. Being able to play the newest high-speed video game and to watch a movie on a flat-panel television are luxuries, not necessities, and therefore, their deflationary effects really have a limited place in the calculation of the inflation index. The inflation index should be based on the things which we require, and on which the bulk of our money is spent.

At this point, a very important question begs to be asked. If the ever-increasing speed and power of computers were truly deflationary, wouldn't they be driving down the costs of everything else? This concept is so important that it needs to be repeated: IF THE EVER-INCREASING SPEED AND POWER OF COMPUTERS WERE TRULY DEFLATIONARY, WOULDN'T THEY BE DRIVING DOWN THE COSTS OF EVERYTHING ELSE? This is what would truly occur if, in fact, these items were "deflationary". Unfortunately, this does not appear to be happening, and the reasons are very clear. Many of these products have little effect on controlling inflation, and therefore their "deflationary" effects are vastly overstated.

When I put pen to paper and calculate what I believe to be a "real" inflation rate, I arrive at a rate over the last few years of approximately 5% to 7% per year. I refer to my brand of inflation interchangeably as "real inflation" or "stealth inflation", the latter because it appears to be off the Fed's radar. But make no mistake. It is there, it has been there for several years, and it is very real.

Even if we very badly wanted to pretend that there was very little inflation, we couldn't do it for long. The unemployment rate has gotten back down to below levels generally considered full employment, and commodity prices present a compelling story which simply cannot be ignored. For the three-year period ending 2005, most measures of commodity indexes had risen by over 50%. The stated inflation rate over this same period, however, was less than 10%. Clearly something has to give. Either the Fed will have to reign in this commodity inflation before it becomes fully reflected in prices for everyday items, or it will have a massive inflation problem on its hands, and will have to take much more drastic measures later on.

Debt and Inflation

I have spent considerable time analyzing how rising, falling, and stagnant levels of debt and inflation have affected the US stock market over the last century. Of all the major combinations I have studied, the one with the worst effect on the stock market has been the combination of rising government debt with rising inflation.

It should come as no surprise that the US economy is faced with such a situation at this time, yet the stock market has surprisingly been on the rise. The reason this combination is bad for the stock market is somewhat complicated for those who are not well versed in economics, but I will attempt to briefly summarize why this is so. When the government has high levels of debt and the rate of debt growth is increasing, it must borrow more and more money to fund the debt. Because inflation is also rising, the government must increase interest rates not only to attract investors for taking on added risk, but also to vanquish inflation by slowing down the economy. The government's higher interest rates in turn pressure other lenders to increase their interest rates to remain competitive. As the war of interest rates is waged, forces can push the government to raise short-term rates to levels higher than long-term rates, resulting in an inverted yield curve. When the yield curve inverts, there is a very high risk that the economy may enter a recessionary period, and along with that, a stock market correction.

Yield Curve Inversion

One of the most talked about and closely observed relationships is that of the yield curve. A typical yield curve shows the relationship between yields on Treasuries versus time. We have an inverted yield curve when this curve slopes downward with time rather than upward. When the yield curve inverts, short-term rates exceed long-term rates. Some economists and analysts watch the spread (the difference in yield between varying lengths of Treasuries) and compute a likelihood of recession over an ensuing period of time based on the spread and on historical data. But history is only a guide, and no two situations are identical.

Because we are in a period of understated inflation, accompanied by negative savings rates and large deficits, an inverted yield curve may be far more dangerous this time than it has been in the past. As such, if a model suggests a 25% likelihood of recession in the ensuing months, it may need to be adjusted by some multiple, perhaps two or three, which might give a 50% or 75% likelihood of recession. I don't know what this multiple should be. I only know that a multiple should be used. For this reason, I believe that this time around, the slightest inversion is far more ominous a sign than it has been in the majority of inversions in the past, and should be taken very seriously. If I see this and you see this, then the great minds of Wall Street and the Fed must see this. The difference is that they are not going to tell you what I am willing to tell you.

Yield Curve/Stock Market Relationship

A beautiful graph was put out by the Board of the Federal Reserve System show-ing the relationship between the 10-year T-note and the fed-funds rate (the spread) versus the annualized quarterly percentage change in inflation-adjusted GDP. It shows what happened to the economy each quarter in relation to the spread, going back to the early 1960's. Such information permits an observer to see which period the current situation most resembles, and gives a sense of what might occur going forward. The yield curve inverted significantly in the late 1960's, in the mid 1970's, and in the late 1970's. Each steep inversion was accompanied by corrections in the Dow of approximately 25%, 35%, and 45%, respectively. It also shows that these inversions followed periods of extraordinarily high adjusted rates of change in GDP (anywhere from 5% to 10%) which were accompanied by high oil prices.

Since the 1980's, the Fed has tightened short-term rates each time adjusted GDP growth approached 5%, and the yield curve did not experience such drastic inversions as in the prior decades. However, the combination of fear of steep inversions, along with twin deficits, highly valued stock markets and real estate markets, and fear of the erosion of US economic might, accompanied by a slight inversion, all contributed to the stock market crash of October, 1987. Assuming that Greenspan and Bernanke can successfully navigate through similar issues, significant market corrections might be averted. But the investor must be aware that corrections of similar magnitude could occur in the current environment. Today's yield curve thus far most resembles the pattern of the early 1990's, which was accompanied by relatively steady GDP growth and only a slight stock market correction, so it is certainly possible that there could be a repeat of that scenario. But two things the early 90's period was missing were sky high real estate prices and immense global competition for oil, which leads to inflation. I believe that we are more likely to experience a significant stock market correction than a min-imal one very soon, and if market cycles have their way, we could be looking at one as early as the Spring of 2006, but certainly no later than by the Fall of 2007.

Let's take a closer look at interest rate changes in recent cycles and see how they compare with today's changes. In October, 1987, the Fed raised interest rates and the stock market crashed. Greenspan then abruptly lowered rates to sta-bilize the markets before he resumed tightening to 10%. He then embarked on a three-year downshift from 10% to 3%, before raising rates again. We now find ourselves in a very similar period. Summarizing for the two periods gives the fol-lowing information (these numbers are approximations):

Time Period	1989 to 1992	2001 to 2003
Change in Rates	10% to 3%	6.5% to 1%
Change of Rates in Points	-7	-5.5
Change of Rates in %	-70%	-85%

Time Period	1993 to 1995	2003 to 2006
Change in Rates	3% to 6%	1% to 5%
Change of Rates in Points	3	4
Change of Rates in %	100%	500%

I might be tempted to say that a repeat of the bull market of 1995 to 1999 was in store, but for one critical factor. In the 1990's, interest rates had come up only 100%. This time they are coming up 500%! Something that many pundits do not realize is that both measures of magnitude of change in interest rates and percentage change in interest rates are significant psychologically and in real terms. Generally the measure of change in magnitude would be the more significant of the two as it would be the one which consumers actually feel in their ability to spend, but this time is truly different. With a zero savings rate, even the smallest change in magnitude will be felt, and a significant change in percentage terms becomes more meaningful than ever simply because it is felt more on a relative basis. As these rate increases work their way through the system, borrowers will have "sticker shock" when they see some of their debt interest rates rise by as much as a couple hundred percent. This is the sort of change in interest rates that can stop an economy in its tracks.

An entire book could be written on the interactions between debt, inflation, the yield curve, and the stock market, so at this point it's probably best to leave off with this brief summary of some of the dynamics at work.

Commodity Prices and Inflation

Commodity prices give a lot of information about inflation, and more importantly, about future inflation. Wherever one looks, almost all measurements of commodities prices are giving the same signs (recall, the index was up about 50% over a recent 3-year period). Inflation is here, it is reflected in the prices of commodities, and it is trending higher. I'm quite certain the Fed is watching this, and as long as inflation continues to show itself in the prices of commodities, do not expect the Fed to discontinue its policy of increasing interest rates. A main role of the Fed is inflation fighter, and this indicator is flashing bright red warning signals.

Labor Costs

Wage and salary increases have held fairly steady throughout the last 20 years, fluctuating between yearly rates of increase of approximately 2.5% and 5%. Health insurance cost increases, however, have fluctuated wildly, coming from north of 15% annually in the early 1980's down to 4% in 1986, back up to 15% by 1988, down to zero in 1996, and in recent years back up over 10% with no slowdown in sight. The bull market of the late 1990's can be partially attributed to the lower rates of increase during that period.

With wage and salary cost increases fairly steady over the most recent 20-year period, a relationship between health insurance cost increases and the stock market is evident. When rates of health insurance cost increases came down to mid-single digits in 1986 and 1987, the stock market soared. As increases crossed 10%, things got rough. Finally, when rates of increases fell below 5% again in 1995, the market began its upward climb, and continued through 2000 when an increase over 8% coincided with major market corrections. Although the markets have since rebounded, they have not attained their prior heights, and with health insurance rates of increases holding steady at 10%, it is unlikely the market climb can continue. Given that health insurance costs make up an ever-increasing percentage of total worker compensation, future percentage increases in health insurance costs will have an ever-increasing proportional impact on company profitability. I would venture to say that the markets will not break through their prior highs convincingly until health insurance cost increases come back down to below 5%, while salary and wage increases are held in the 2 to 5% range.

I do not intend for my analysis to imply that health insurance costs determine the direction of the stock market. I am implying, however, that they are a factor, along with inflation in general, interest rates, debt, and all the other forces which can and do impact the investment markets.

Labor Shortage

I always read about this labor shortage or that labor shortage. One of the most irritating labor shortages I read about is the engineering labor shortage. I have been hearing about this one on and off for 30 years. My high school guidance counselor persuaded me to become an engineer by using this argument (he sexed it up a bit by suggesting I could be serving my country in the cold war with Russia or in the then oncoming economic war with Japan). Today, I can hardly open a paper or listen to a talk show that isn't promoting the current "shortage". I wonder how this can be when I know of highly competent engineers who have either left the engineering profession because they couldn't get work, or are working in positions paying low salaries in relation to what people in "high finance" might be earning. All a company would have to do is cut a few executives' salaries by marginal amounts, allocate that money to recruiting engineers, and they would suddenly have no problem finding that critical engineer. Ah, but what they really mean is that they cannot find an engineer with all the expertise they desire at the low salary they wish to pay him/her. And who can blame them? Why should they sacrifice their compensation when nobody is demanding that they do so? If they can hold out and plead to the government, perhaps the government will relax the immigration laws so that more technically qualified immigrants can remain in or enter the country. Or better still, they could offshore the work to China or India to keep the costs even lower. And even if a company's executives didn't think about things this way, the impatient controlling investors are thinking this way, and if the executives in question wish to keep their jobs, they had better comply with the wishes of their masters.

Now that we understand the dynamics involved in the "labor shortage" we can move on to important, related questions. If there is a "labor shortage" of engineers with hard to find skills (which there actually is in many cases), then why aren't these engineers paid more money. And if there is no shortage of people who are willing to work in hedge funds and mutual funds (work that is far less difficult than engineering), then why are these people paid so much money? In many cases, the executives have even managed to convince the engineers that the engineers do not need as much money as the finance and marketing people. I recall a conversation I had with another engineer at GE, while we were working on the design of the most advanced aircraft engine in the world in the late 1980's. I voiced my objections that we were doing all the heavy lifting while finance people were making as much or more than us in compensation. He proceeded to explain to me that we were getting benefits like not having to wear nice clothes, and therefore we didn't require as much money. He really believed this!

My example of engineers is in no way meant to convey that engineers are superior to other professionals. I use it because I was an engineer, and there have been many articles concerning the subject recently. Similar arguments can be made for scientists, programmers, doctors, nurses, teachers, and many others whose services are specialized and critical.

Consumer Sentiment, Consumer Spending, and the Stock Market

Consumer spending drives the economy. Estimates are that the consumer accounts for two-thirds of GDP in the US. So it behooves the investor to closely watch consumer sentiment. Studying data over the last few decades has allowed me to make the following observations:

1. When sentiment either rises rapidly or is sustained above normal levels, retail sales rise.

2. When sentiment falls below a given level for a given period of time, sales suffer.

3. When rates of sales increases peak at 10%, sharp reversals of fortune tend to follow.

4. Coincident plunges in sentiment and sales are very bad.

Number 1 generally describes the US environment of the past few years, through the hurricane season of 2005 (as the wealth effect of the stock market and/or real estate market made people happy and confident). Number 3 suggests caution, as the retail industry is coming off a period of very high sales growth rates. The plunge in sentiment in September, 2005 to about 75, represented the lowest level in over a decade and the steepest decline in several decades.

Prevailing sentiment levels of the 1970's coincided with a series of significant stock market corrections which would last into the early 80's. Much of the final outcome this time around will depend even more on the magnitude and sustainability of declines in consumer sentiment, as the consumer now accounts for a greater percentage of US spending than at any time in recent history. The wise would be very cautious.

Supply Management Index

The US has clearly transitioned to a services economy in the past few decades. While the manufacturing component of the economy will never completely disappear, it is truly a shadow of its former self. As this transition has been exacerbated in recent years, it is more important than ever to gage the health of the economy by monitoring the health of the services component of the economy. And when the Institute for Supply Management's US non-manufacturing index falls below 50, the economy could be in trouble. After enjoying a move from slightly below 50 in early 2003 to about 70 in January 2005, the index experienced a rapid falloff, heading towards 50 in 2005. Investors may be too optimistic. Once these numbers start falling, they often don't bottom until getting below 50 in the midst of recession, and recessions are usually accompanied by stock market corrections.

The China Syndrome

Many US consumers owe a great debt (literally) to the Chinese. I recommend that everyone who has benefited from an interest-only mortgage or a low adjustable- or even a long-term fixed-rate mortgage send a letter of thanks to the Chinese government. They have made many dream homes possible, but I regret to inform these proud homeowners that one day, the Chinese may take that very home from their sons and daughters. For someone who has little savings and little home equity, and who recently bought a home in an overheated market, it is important to understand that the Chinese made this possible by being one of the biggest lenders to the US. Unfortunately this state of affairs won't continue forever. There will come a point when lenders (foreigners) to the US will demand higher interest rates to compensate them for their investment risk, or they may demand higher rates simply because they can.

To illustrate the power the Chinese may have over the US consumer someday, let's look at the history of a company like Microsoft (MSFT). Each time MSFT entered a new market dominated by another company, it offered its competing product free or at much lower cost (this is essentially what the Chinese do with their goods and with their loans). Often in as little as a year or two, MSFT would get a lock on the market for this new product and wipe out the competition (this is also what China does). Once the competition had capitulated, absent government intervention, MSFT would raise its prices or at least hold its prices steady for products and services. The Chinese can also eventually do this through price increases, or worse, by refusing to fund US deficits, and thereby forcing interest rates to rise rapidly. Indeed, from 2000 through 2005, there had been over an 80% increase in the amount of foreign holdings of US Treasury and US mortgage-backed bonds. For those who believe I am exaggerating, just imagine a scenario 50 years from now in which the US economy is slipping into the economic abyss and the Chinese foreclose on 25% of US homes. The US government could ask the Chinese to give US citizens some slack, but at that point the Chinese would probably have reached their limit and would demand repayment in cash or in hard assets (i.e. the homes). The US government could intervene by telling the Chinese that if they continued down this path, they would risk war. Unfortunately, however, 50 years from now, it is very possible that the Chinese military will be more powerful than that of the US, and the US government could not do much to help its citizens. At that point much of US citizenry would come to know what it feels like to be dominated by a foreign power.

This scenario need not occur. All it takes is for the US consumer to wizen up. This means to stop living on debt, and to start saving instead of spending.

Technology Lead Slipping

The US edge in technology may be fading. In recent years, US corporations have outsourced lots of technology manufacturing and services. While this helps corporations make money in the short term, it also gives US technology to other nations. These nations, churning out engineers at breathtaking rates, can now build on outsourced US intellectual property and may eventually overtake the US. Did I say eventually?

Numbers from the Commerce Department put the US negative trade balance in advanced technology goods in 2004 at a level equal to its greatest surplus from the early 1990's, when it dominated advanced technology goods trade. For the short-term benefit of helping the stocks of a few companies, the US has turned over much of the control of technology to the rest of the world. And those who control technology and information will ultimately control the finances of the world, and possibly the world itself. The point is that there are strong indications that the US economy could enter a period where it falls behind its chief rivals in growth and power, which are beginning to look increasingly like China and India. These nations will stumble along the way, but a trend has been put in place, and if that trend proceeds unchecked, it may become irreversible.

Market Valuations and Returns

Two common measures of stock market valuation can give a lot of information about where the markets stand in relation to prior periods and where they might be heading in the future. Figures in the following table show that a recent

S&P500 price earnings ratio (P/E) puts valuations somewhere in the middle of record lows and record highs for the last several decades (these are approximate figures which were generated based on prevailing numbers from the many different methods—GAAP, pro forma, hybrids—of calculating these ratios). Total market capitalization as a percentage of Gross Domestic Product (GDP) also falls somewhere in the middle of a recent range. Based on these numbers, one might be tempted to say the market is fairly priced, but this type of thinking would be to ignore that the cycle of lower interest rates has ended, and that the future will bring either flat or increasing interest rates. Factoring in interest rate issues, it is more likely that valuations will gravitate towards 1982 numbers than towards 1999/2000 numbers.

	S&P500 P/E @ Peak	Market Cap/GDP @ Peak
2005/2006	25	125%
1999/2000	45	180%
1982	10	35%

The S&P500 price earnings ratio reached peaks of approximately 30 or higher three times in US medium- to long-term history. This occurred around 1895, then again about 1930, and most recently in early 2000. By now most people realize that the US stock market experienced something in the late 1990's which it is not likely to experience again in our lifetimes. A more likely scenario is hitting the once-in-a-generation high P/E of 30 upon completion of the next hypergrowth cycle. An investor, therefore, must throw out all the stock market data from 1999/2000 as a gross aberration, and use all the other data available in order to make rational decisions in the future. The price earnings ratio hit lows in the range of 5 to 10 three times in the 1900's. Each of these lows set off the three great bull markets of that century (the 1920's, the 1950's/60's, and the 1980's/90's). History has shown repeatedly that the ratio needs to fall to the single digits once again prior to setting things up for the first great bull market of the new century. The key to understanding the markets, once again, is not to get lost in the minutiae, but rather to observe the trends and cycles.

Many pundits attempt to persuade the investor how undervalued or fairly valued the market is, with an essential goal in mind. That goal is to get the investor to put more money into the market, or at least not to take any away from it. They might show a hypothetical study in which the P/E of a stock, sector, or market is extremely attractive based on recent history.

Well, here's some more news for them.

Data shows that recent ten-year average P/E's of trailing earnings of the S&P500 are higher than at any time in a century, except for 1999 and 1929. This means that it is even higher than it was at its peak in the 1960's, after which time the market went into a 16-year period of stagnation. Granted the stock market is unlikely to experience another 1929 or 2000-type swoon in terms of severity and longevity, but nothing indicates that it will escape a 1960's/70's-type situation marked by several short-term cycles resulting in medium-term stagnation. Of course, however, such a climate is perfect for astute market timers, as they will use the long-term investor as ballast.

Market Dividends and Returns

Something very unusual occurred in the mid to late 1990's. For the first time, the dividend yield on the S&P500 broke through 3% in a sustained fashion to the down side, and continued down to a yield of a mere 1% by the year 2000. This was previously unheard of, but it is another reason why the rally of the 90's went on for so long. Many "knowledgeable" market participants (myself included) became skeptical of the rally when the 3% barrier was broken to the down side, but as the market continued its upward run while the yield fell lower still, many investors who had sidelined themselves needed to become participants in the run-up for fear of being left behind. It was almost as if a "short squeeze" was taking place, and the market was driven higher and higher as all the holdouts came in. The game then became to figure out when to get out. The rest is history.

Here we are in 2006, and the yield is slowly clawing its way back up towards the 3% level. An astute investor might wonder how she is supposed to know what an appropriate dividend yield might be. The history of dividend yields might help to make such a determination. There had been an interesting long-term trend in place from the early 1900's, during which time the yield fluctuated between 3% and higher figures, which peaked at about 10% (excluding the early 1930's), and then effectively sloped downward as time moved toward the year 2000. At the start of each major bull market in the 1900's, the yield started at some local peak and worked its way down to the 3% baseline, which routinely signaled the end of each major bull market. I believe the breakdown of this cycle in the 1990's was an aberration, and before a new major bull market can begin, the yield will not only have to break through the magical 3% level to the upside, but will have to work its way up to some new peak level, much the way it did at the start of the previous century. Of course there will be plenty of trading opportunities between now and then, but another major bull market is unlikely until all the necessary conditions are in place. As support for my claims, the yield fell from an average of about 8% to 3% during each of the bull markets of the 1920's and 1950's. Similarly in its dissimilarity, the yield fell from 6% to 1% in the 1980's/90's, helping to power that massive bull market rally.

Volatility Indexes

The VIX and the VXN are two common volatility indexes for the US stock markets.

When volatility is low, that's good, right? WRONG!

Contrary to popular opinion, low volatility does not equate with low risk. It does, however, equate with investor complacency. Normally investors are complacent when the market is slowly moving up or treading in place, without many days of wide moves in either direction. This is precisely when the danger flags should be waving, because it signifies that a move is coming soon, and when volatility indexes are at lows, this stock market move is often downward. Of course the people who want the investor to put his money into the market will rarely explain this, perhaps barring a few exceptions. They may say it's a good time to invest because some sort of nirvana has been reached, where volatility is unlikely to be seen again, implying that the markets are now safe.

Changes in volatility can mean lots of things. For instance, the number of days in 2005 when the S&P 500 index rose or fell by more than 1% was about 30 versus four times that amount in 2002, while in 1995 there were only about a dozen such days. Someone who watches trends might believe volatility is at a bottom, and ready to move upward, while another person might believe the current trend should continue. We however, realize that nothing can be concluded from one or two trends alone, and that the entire picture must be observed in detail before making a judgment. As it turns out, there may now be very good reasons for not making abrupt judgments.

While the index has shown relatively less volatility, I am observing a great deal of volatility in individual stocks. A big reason for this could be a combination of events. First, as more investors have decided to index their investments, active traders pile in and out of individual stocks to drive those stocks up and down, and in the process make money while the indexes go nowhere. Second, the lower capital gains tax rate makes such trading more profitable in after-tax dollars. A savvy trader will wait for the big guys to drive a stock down, and then buy it at a local low with a one-year commitment. Assuming it goes up over the next 12 months and that trader sells, a measly tax rate of only 15% is applied to that gain. This suddenly becomes a very attractive way to make a living. If this same trader was working in a salaried position, his/her tax rate could be more than double the 15% rate (it should also be noted that more trading equals less productivity in the economy, as this trading contributes very little, if anything to society). As I explained earlier in the book, the typical buy and hold investor has served the trader very well, for this investor has provided ballast for the trader. In many of these situations, the trader can make 50% or even 200% on his money over a given one-year period, while for the buy and hold investor who is in for the long haul, a gain may never materialize.

In addition to all the current stock market complacency, there is also unusual complacency in the bond market. High-yield corporate and emerging market bond spreads over US Treasury bonds have normally been considerable (historically, generally from 5 to 15 percentage points), in order to compensate investors for their added risk. By 2005, the spread for these risky securities had fallen to the 2% range. Historically, when spreads on these instruments fall to levels greater than where they currently are, the bond and/or stock markets have been dealt serious set-backs. Considering that those levels have been breached, I believe the market is behaving somewhat euphorically (beyond complacent) in allowing these types of spreads and volatility numbers to be maintained for such a long period of time, and that the governing forces will soon bring a day of reckoning.

Bond Defaults

Corporate bond defaults always accompany any major stock market correction, so a prudent investor should keep an eye on the bond market. Peaks in risky borrowing and lending generally indicate a market top. The top pros watch these numbers closely, but it is likely that nobody is giving the small investor this information. Word on the street is that the average lower junk debt default period is only a few years from the time of issuance. Interestingly, late 2004 set the recent record for high-yield junk-bond issuance. Wall Street's salespeople and funds which specialize in holding such high-yield junk are likely not to disclose to the small investor that a record in junk issuance has been set. Most likely they will give the investor a prospectus which warns of the risks (which unfortunately nobody takes seriously because it is usually accompanied by many warnings as required by the regulatory agencies) without raising any warning flags directly.

Based on historic trends, if junk issuance does not climb higher than the levels set in 2004, one can assume that default rates will peak around 2007 in the current cycle. This implies that defaults will start happening very soon in order to work their way up to that peak. It is probably a good idea to stay away from any long-term investments in junk-rated companies going forward for a period of time. As the next cycle approaches, it could be a good time once again to enter this market.

Cash Held By Corporations

Cash held by corporations can tell us a lot about how corporate executives feel markets may behave in the future. Figures show the amount of cash held by S&P 500 corporations has risen exponentially in recent decades to over $600 billion. Much of this is due to the easy money created by extended periods of low interest rates, along with an extended period of low dividend yields and increased efficiency and profitability. The current level of cash held suggests the market could be entering a slow-growth period, during which time a substantial portion of company profits are made from cash earning interest from financial investments. If, in fact, this is how the S&P 500 companies will be using that cash, then what is the justification for paying their management exorbitant compensation to do what investors could be doing themselves?

On a closely related subject, payroll outsourcing companies had been reporting fantastic earnings increases, and the less informed investor might believe that these increases were being generated by improvements in business operations. The truth is, however, that as interest rates rise rapidly, these companies make increasing amounts of money off the "float" (the time that they have their clients' money and they earn interest on it before they pay it out to the tax authorities). Stock brokerage companies have been getting similar benefits by keeping clients' cash in low-yielding accounts, while collecting healthy interest for themselves. In all cases, this money goes straight to the bottom line, making these companies appear as though they have found a new way of growing. The truth is that when rates stop rising, so too will the increased interest rate contribution to their bottom lines.

Buybacks

What's a company that's sitting on a pile of cash with few growth prospects or attractive acquisition targets to do? Buy back its stock, of course. This allows the company to reinvest in itself by reducing the number of shares outstanding and thereby increasing the value per share, right?

Normally there is a high likelihood this would be correct, but this time it's different. This time a lot of companies are announcing buybacks, hoping to lure in or retain unsuspecting shareholders who are likely unaware of what may truly be happening. First, many announced, planned buybacks are just that—"announced", planned buybacks. Many of them are never fully completed. But more of a concern is the recent trend of companies buying back their own shares to cover stock compensation for their executives and other key employees. On the surface, while buybacks may sound like a good thing, it is important to understand the entire financial situation of each company making such an announcement. Companies are buying back stock in a big way, with S&P500 Index companies spending about twice as much in 2005 as they did in 2003. While this is generally considered good for shareholder value, the details of each situation must be analyzed on its own merits. With new rules scheduled to go into effect in 2006 concerning the expensing of stock options, there is bound to be plenty of turmoil in the markets.

Profits and Spending

Companies in the S&P500 are making more money than ever, but capital spending hasn't kept pace. Numbers from Standard & Poor's show that in mid-2000 companies were earning about $110 billion per quarter and spending about $750 billion, and by mid-2005 they were earning about $160 billion and spending only about $800 billion. In other words, the ratio of spending to earning fell by about 30%. This is a very significant difference, and might be accounted for by many factors, among them, overspending that may have continued into 2002, a tax plan that rewards cashing out by owners and executives, and outsourcing to low-cost countries. Whatever the reasons, the potential exists for long term declining health of these companies, as capital spending is the best indicator of reinvestment, and perhaps ultimately of the long-term sustainability of a company's superiority over its competitors. Investors should be thinking about whether companies' long-term health is being sacrificed for the short term, and how this might affect the long-term investor. Another possible reason for the relative decrease in spending could be that company executives believe that the market is at a cycle high, and they may be hoarding cash in anticipation of a coming bear market. This could be looked upon as responsible leadership on their parts, but unfortunately it doesn't do much for the long-term shareholder.

Stock Market Leads

What I have known for a good many years is that the stock market leads the economy. Much of this relationship is due to the expectations and actions of the savviest and most powerful investors. In regard to expectations, the savviest investors have studied and experienced market behavior, and with that, how the market responds to its own growth and to changes in interest rates, among other factors. These investors do not wait for the future to arrive, but forecast the future based on past cycles, and then attempt to beat the future to the punch. If the economy is going strong, and companies and stocks are performing well, the assumption is that soon interest rates will rise. When this occurs, the market and the economy hit a soft patch. The savvy investors will time the market cycle, cash in their chips at or near the market top, and get ready to re-enter the market following the anticipated correction.

This brings us to the results of these savviest investors' actions. Their actions of selling positions near the market top confirm the market correction. As the Fed begins raising interest rates to cool the economy, these investors begin to sell. They halt the market's rise and contribute to its decline, as selling pressure increases. As the market starts to fall, other investors panic and also sell, further contributing to the fall. These savvy investors closely follow the actions of the market and the economy, and anticipate the next Fed moves in regard to interest rate policy, and then again, attempt to beat the future to the punch by getting back into the market at local lows.

Of course, another interesting thing happens along the way. The decline in the market plays to the "wealth effect". Companies and consumers no longer feel as wealthy as they did when the market was rising, and because of this, they tend to tighten up on spending. Just a little tightening up on spending can go a long way, causing company revenues and profits to fall, in turn, greatly affecting individual stock prices, the overall market, and the numbers for the economy. The Fed sees this development taking place, halts the rising of interest rates, and soon begins to lower rates to re-stimulate the economy. Understanding this cycle, the savvy investor always tries to get out in front of it.

Movements of the Dow and the S&P500 over the last century confirm that when earnings are soaring, the stock market is hardly up, on average, yet when earnings are falling considerably, stock markets can soar. To be expected, when earnings are in free-fall, the market is also in free-fall. This is the result of forces involved in extreme bear markets which extend over a few years like the 1929 to 1932 period and also during the period of 2000 to 2003, when market collapses and decreasing earnings act to reinforce one another and perpetuate continued mutual declines.

These trends are perhaps the most important information available to investors, because to some extent it takes emotion out of the investing equation. When earnings are up huge, be very careful, and when earnings are down some, there is potentially great opportunity. Whatever the earnings climate, the real trick is in using all available data to always be a few steps ahead of the market.

Price Earnings Ratios

The price earnings ratio (P/E) is a common tool used to assign valuation to a stock, market sector, or stock index. It is a measure of market capitalization divided by earnings over a period of time, generally the most recent twelve-month period. Many analysts use the forward P/E as a method of estimating value over the ensuing twelve-month period. My personal belief is that the reason they do this is that a forward P/E is only an estimate which is usually based on a rosy forecast. Should that forecast turn out to be accurate, the analyst looks like a star, and if that forecast turns out to be overly optimistic, the analyst can claim that the bad call was due to "factors" outside of his/her control. It's truly a wonderful system for the analysts and for the companies which employ the analysts.

Although P/E's alone cannot really tell us as much as we wish that they could, they can be meaningful when the economy is in steady-state growth over a large number of years. Too bad history has shown that this is rarely, if ever the case. So at best, P/E's can be used for relative valuation techniques to compare stocks, market sectors or indexes. They can also be useful as part of the price-earnings-to-growth ratio (PEG) which divides the P/E for the trailing twelve-month period by the projected median rate of earnings growth over the coming three-to-five-year period. This helps to normalize the P/E and allows for easier comparative valuations of companies in different industries.

The reader should always remember that stocks and other financial assets never exist in a vacuum, but rather are heavily influenced by the market forces which can and do affect them all.

Taxes

The premise of the current government's tax policy is that lower tax rates will eventually lead to lower deficits. Ah, if only it really worked this way. We have gone from the time of Ronald Reagan, who some would call a genius (while it's unlikely he was a genius, he did possess the intuition to listen to some very intelligent advisors) to our present situation.

Reagan's advisors were able to see that extremely high tax rates were harming growth in the economy. This is because tax rates were so high that potentially high producers rationalized that it did not make sense to work their lives away while almost all of their earnings went to the government. I can certainly understand this as a person who has always worked hard, but would be somewhat less inclined to do so if I would only get to keep a small portion of my earnings. If everyone reacted in such a way, productivity would decrease and revenue collected by the government would also decrease, as fewer and fewer people would be willing to put in the extra energy to keep a smaller and smaller percentage of their earnings (not that dissimilar to a socialist society). This would lead to many ill effects in the economy. In recent decades, the continued trend of lowering tax rates (along with falling interest rates) encouraged a productivity boom and led to an environment in which earnings soared in all sectors of the economy, leading to increased government revenue.

Like all things in life, however, there comes a point of diminishing returns. When billionaires (earning hundreds of millions a year) are taxed at essentially the same rates as people earning a few hundred thousand dollars a year, the point of diminishing returns has likely been reached. The billionaires have all the money they or their offspring could ever hope to use. And with tax rates almost as low as they have been in three-quarters of a century, ultra-high earners see these times as an opportunity to pay themselves rather than to pass the increased earnings on to their subordinates or to hire more workers. In fact, typical business executives will rationalize that it makes sense to outsource their subordinates' work to a low-cost country so that they can earn more themselves while tax rates are low.

If, on the other hand, taxes went back up to somewhere between where they are now and where they were after Reagan reduced them, a more rational situation might exist. People would still be motivated to earn more money for themselves so they could move up the economic ladder, and executives would have less of a reason to steer even more money into their pockets at the expense of their workers and shareholders, as the net benefits after taxes would not be as perverse as they were before. This would likely result in increased wages for the working class, more hiring in the US, and less outsourcing of jobs to low-cost nations. The economy might even grow more rapidly, as the working class would have more money to spend and the extremely wealthy would never stop spending anyway.

For anyone who doubts how the tax system has changed things, numbers are floating around suggesting that the top ½% of earners are pulling in double the percent of earnings they did relative to the rest of the population of just a few decades ago. And this makes perfect sense. If someone is in a position to control how much they earn, and taxes are low, they have a special incentive to ensure that they earn more money now while the tax bite is lower. If the high earner waits a couple of years to cash in, it may be too late, as by then taxes might have risen back to prior levels.

The current tax system creates one additional problem which could turn out to be a total disaster. The middle class and the lower-income earners really got very little on a relative basis from the recent tax cuts. And the continued cost cutting and outsourcing has had the effect of freezing their real wages in place. But with the real rate of inflation rising approximately 5 to 7% per year (based on my analysis) in recent years, these people are forced to find other sources of income. This is where the housing market and debt comes into play. People see that housing prices are rising rapidly and they want to get in on this market before their chances of owning a home slip away forever. With temporarily relaxed lending standards and low interest rates, they get their homes. As the homes appreciate, they treat those homes like ATM's, getting cash and credit from the equity in their homes. This creates a false wealth effect and results in a negative savings rate. Eventually the music stops playing and this all comes back to bite them hard.

I've heard that if all the pages that make up the US tax code were stacked, they would be several feet high. There are well over 60,000 pages in that code. I have no idea of the exact number of pages nor of their true height when stacked, but I do know that a code that lengthy must have numerous areas where the boundaries are very fuzzy, and I do know that the more money an entity has at its disposal, the more affordable its army of top-notch attorneys and accountants becomes. Many entities in industries with limited disclosure obligations can continuously push the boundaries, risking that the fuzziness of the tax code and environment of lax regulation will allow their activities to remain undiscovered (recall Enron, WorldCom, Tyco, Adelphia, and hundreds of others that didn't make the news, but nevertheless were public companies, and still managed to rob us of our hard-earned money). Hedge funds in particular can take advantage if they wish to, by setting up various types of complicated strategies which can defer or accelerate gains, and maybe even create gains where there are none, or make gains disappear. Nobody knows, and strangely I think the government may be afraid of knowing, because knowing could potentially create more instability than not knowing. In all fairness though, the Spitzer contagion is spreading and other regulators have been stepping up to the plate lately (to some extent).

I don't mean to single out hedge funds, because precedent had been set by the large accounting firms. Following the collapse of Arthur Andersen, the US was left with only a few large accounting firms. Many of them were thought to be pushing the envelope, but Andersen got caught shredding documents. As there are only a few such firms to audit the thousands of large, publicly held companies, what were the regulatory authorities to do?

Tax Considerations for the Individual Investor

Taxes are always an important consideration when one invests in the financial markets. And when overall returns are in the low single-digits per year, taxes become even more of a consideration, as do management fees, because they can eat up a greater percent of total return. Investors in mutual funds need to be aware of after-tax returns versus stated returns. This is because many funds are not very tax-efficient and engage in lots of short-term trading. As an example, if a fund reports a 10% gain for the year, and all of that gain comes on short-term trades, an investor could end up with a net return more on the order of 6%, depending on where that investor resides. A fund which gets the bulk of its gains from dividends and long-term capital gains can give an investor a larger after-tax return than a less tax-efficient fund, even though its pre-tax return may be lower. Further, the after-tax return obtained from a fund should always be compared to the after-tax return that could be earned in a risk-free money-market fund to assess whether the return is worth the risk. As an example, in 2006, a New York City resident will earn more than 3% on a triple tax-free money-market fund. This risk-free return should be compared to the after-tax return of any other investment under consideration.

Investors who trade stocks also need to pay special attention to prevailing capital gains tax rates. With long-term rates at 15%, simply holding a stock for an extra week or month could mean the difference of paying 15% versus 30% in taxes. An investor might decide to do all his short-term trading in a retirement account, where there is no tax consequence on trades until the money is withdrawn from the account, and to do all his long-term trading (over a one-year holding period) in a taxable account to take advantage of the lower tax rate. Likewise, if an investor wants to hold cash in a high-yielding money-market fund, that investor may want to do so in an IRA or other retirement account where the income is not taxed until withdrawn. Similarly, it might be best to hold dividend-paying stocks in taxable accounts, where those dividends are currently taxed at the low rate of 15%. If everything is carefully planned, investors can as much as double their after-tax returns without taking on any additional risk. Unfortunately, very few planners and brokers will take the time to explain all this to a client, because it can be very time consuming, and as we all know, time is money.

Insider Selling

Historically, when insiders sell large quantities of stock relative to what they buy, watch out. The critical ratio of sellers to buyers varies along with who one talks to. Much of the data available brings me to the conclusion that when the ratio hits a low of 5 for a period of time, the market has bottomed, and on the other hand, when the ratio hits 20 the market is in danger territory and a market top is imminent. Recent studies are attempting to justify why the ratios have been so much higher than 20 for an extended period with no resulting market correction. My response to those studies is that an investor should not be persuaded by the "newbies" who try to fit the curve, and now claim that the ratio signifying a danger zone should be raised (they also did this curve fitting in the late 1990's with measurements like "eyeballs" to justify hyper-valued internet stocks). The run-rate in 2005 was about 30, which to me suggests the most dangerous time since 1999 and 2000, when the ratio was in the range of 20 to 25. The ratio was at 30 in 2003 and 2004 as well, after averaging about 5 to 20 in 2001 and 2002. Quickly scanning the data in February, 2006 told me that nosebleed territory had been reached, with ratios in the range of 50 to 100!

There is currently lots of debate on Wall Street over the correct time to sell or buy based on insider sales and purchases. In recent years, with options, restricted shares, lower tax rates, and everything else figuring into the calculations, targets are all over the place. But my own investigations have shown that there appears to be a long-term cycle of stock market bottoms when this ratio gets to an approximate low of 5. It can go to 10, 30, or even 50 as the stock market is climbing, but I would be very hesitant to load up on equity for the long haul until the ratio falls back to around 5. Until it gets back down to that level, the stock market should best be treated as a trading vehicle rather than as a buy and hold investment.

The stock market truly is a zero-sum game. So when others are busy buying and driving the market up, that is the cue to think about selling. Likewise, when the market is being driven down, that is the cue to start thinking about buying. This is why it's very important to watch what's going on at the buyout firms. Buyout firms recently started to greatly outperform the stock market indexes. An investor's goal must be to understand what this means, and what it means is that as usual, the big, smart money is leading the charge. They got in before the masses, when valuations were much lower, and now they are selling at highs.

But the small investor is smarter than they believe she is. The small investor is asking herself why she should buy what the pros are willing to sell. She is also asking why they would even want to sell. After all, wouldn't they want to hold on to these prizes? Why would they want to do a total stranger a favor, and let her in on a great deal? The answers to these last two questions are, respectively, of course and they wouldn't. Only by selling their cast-offs to the small investor will they be able to achieve market beating performance.

Legal Market Manipulation

A stock goes up on good news. Another stock goes up on bad news. A third goes up on no news. Anything can happen any day and any time, despite market trends, and it can happen for a variety of reasons. Traders and investors could be selling or buying on anticipation of news, or on the news, or "shorts" could be getting squeezed. Market participants could be trading because a takeover is pending (and data has always shown that a few privileged people have access to leaked news of a takeover) or for a great number of other reasons. Or stocks could be moving due to what I call "legal market manipulation".

Let's say someone gets word that Warren Buffet (or Carl Icahn, or Kirk Kerkorian, or Fidelity Investments) is buying a position in XYZ corporation. The momentum players and arbitrageurs are sitting and watching their computers for unusual activity, and when they see or hear what they are looking for, they pounce, and join in the fray. It happens far too rapidly for the unconnected investor to play in this game, and usually by the time the average Joe joins in, the move is done. What used to occur before regulation (in the early part of the 1900's) is that the big boys might simply call each other on the phone and find out what each other was doing. Assuming they agreed to act together, that would be considered market manipulation, and would today be illegal. But what happens today is perfectly legal, as nobody (at least I like to think nobody) is necessarily agreeing to act in unison. Today, it's mostly done through electronic monitoring (i.e. the use of computers to instantly track high volume movements and possibly even the source of the movement). So while there is no "insider" trading for all intents and purposes, for the average trader and investor without immediate access to sophisticated tools of the trade, the net result is similar to insider trading, in that those with access to powerful monitoring systems do in fact have a form of inside information (information that is not available to presumably over 99% of market participants). So while it is perfectly legal (i.e. the information is available to everybody in theory), it is not available to 99% of the population, realistically. It therefore may be analogous to insider information.

I must stress, that although it may be immoral and unethical (putting the rest of us at a disadvantage), this type of trading is legal, and therefore is not technically "insider trading". Further, this is not that much different than what goes on in most other industries, in that companies with the best information and/or technology are generally victorious. The difference however is that in those industries the battles are fought between companies, whereas in the case of the investment markets, the battles are waged between companies, and also between companies and individual clients, professionals and companies, and professionals and individuals. It is a very complicated battlefield which leaves the unsophisticated individual investor easily exploited.

Congress

As reported in the New Yorker, October, 31, 2005, Alan Ziobrowski, a professor at Georgia State examined 6000 equity transactions over a 5-year period in the 1990's by US senators. His findings aren't comforting. During this period, the average senator beat the market by 12% per annum. Compare this with corporate insider market out-performance of 6% during that period, and a few eyebrows should be rising. Sure the senators have access to all sorts of non-public information, and plenty of acquaintances in important positions, but they also happen to be a very intelligent group of people, right? Well, I for one am stumped. I'm not even going to attempt to explain this one.

Shorts

There are lots of "shorts" in the market. For those who are unfamiliar with "shorts", they are the people who bet that a stock or index, or anything shorts can trade will go down. If enough of them bet that something will go down, it may actually do so. This can cause people who are "long" a position to sell out of fear that they will incur a loss or lose their gains, which can drive the asset price down further still, possibly even eventually to zero (the CEO of Overstock.com has recently been claiming the shorts are after his company). Obviously, the most thinly traded financial assets are most vulnerable to shorts, as it doesn't take that many shorts to drive such an asset's price down (I am told that the old saying "don't sell yourself short" comes from this practice of selling an asset for less than it may be worth). There are people who make a living out of shorting-only, and of course there are slews of hedge funds which only short, as well as ones that go short and long on various assets, at various times, in various combinations. Just imagine how this might all work out if a few major players got together behind the scenes to short a stock. With 8000 hedge funds out there controlling so much money, it seems there is a high likelihood that discussions take place.

A very dangerous time of the year is during and after the usual October sell-off. Hedge funds, mutual funds, and individual investors are evaluating their portfolios, repositioning themselves for the following year, and harvesting losses for tax strategies. In the middle of all this are the shorts. They can help drive the price of a security down rapidly or they can end up getting "squeezed". They get squeezed when a large buyer or group of buyers starts buying the security they shorted. This forces the shorts to cover and ends up having the inverse effect of driving up the price of the asset. Squeezing is a strategy employed by investors or by groups of investors, as they monitor securities with the largest short positions, and then swoop in for the kill. They might swiftly drive up the price, only to abruptly sell their positions after a tidy gain, allowing the shorts to take control once again. This battle between the shorts and the longs goes on and on, over and over, and for the buy and hold investor who listens to his advisor, it is simply not a winning situation.

Successful short-sellers are among the most adept traders in the game (although on average, they may be net losers). They study all the statistics and they know that the final months of the year are traditionally the strongest for the bulls. With this in mind, once a shorted stock has made some money for the shorts, many of them will bail out of their short positions (taking their gains or cutting their losses) before the bulls pile into these assets to begin the "short squeeze". When this occurs, the few shorts left in a given position will be obliterated by the bulls, and many shorted securities will see significant gains.

Collapsing Stocks

Over the course of a couple of years a stock comes down from 50 to 5. An investor studies the company and finds that it has some issues, but overall its reputation is intact, its revenues are moving up, and it only has to better manage its operations to get its earnings back on track and straighten out its debt situation. In the old days, an established company might have been given a chance to work things out. These days, maybe it will and maybe it won't. After all, controlling investors are an impatient lot who have been made even less patient in this low tax environment which drives them to make as much money as they can as fast as they can, before the tax rules change. And who can blame them? The difference between forcing a company into bankruptcy and taking control now versus waiting for another year or two might in the long run mean the difference of hundreds of millions of dollars in returns for their organizations.

In such an environment, the small investor is more vulnerable than ever. There is so much dealing going on behind the scenes with all the hedge funds, large investors, mutual funds, pension funds, and everyone else that controls the debt and equity of a company, that the small investor has absolutely no way of knowing whether a company on the brink can survive. The best thing to do in such a situation is either to stay away, or if one cannot control oneself, to buy a very small amount of stock which he plans on losing (then he might be pleasantly surprised). Either way, after the wars are waged and winners are determined, the investor can't be too badly hurt. If the investor is a proficient trader, perhaps he can make some money off of some trades, but he should not invest serious money for the long term in an embattled company.

Private-Equity Firms

A disturbing, re-emerging trend has recently surfaced in the financial markets. There is a breed of private-equity firm (PEF) which is willing to go to great lengths to enrich its management and investors. There have been increasing reports that these firms have been engaging in business practices which saddle the companies in their portfolios with massive debts so that the new owners can pay themselves outsized dividends.

Traditionally, a PEF might spot an opportunity, and then take control of a private or public company. In the case of a public company, the PEF would take it private. Without quarterly demands from the public markets, the PEF might take a couple of years to turn the underperforming company around, and then possibly bring the healthy company public once again, earning a tidy profit for itself. The PEF would also make its money off of fees levied on its portfolio of companies for a range of services provided during the turnaround period.

Recently, the range of services for which many PEF's are charging has grown rapidly, along with the fees for those services. But the most sensitive area concerns the outsized dividends which are being paid to some PEF's while their portfolio companies are saddled with so much debt in some cases that many of them may never be turned around, and in the event they are taken public, they would be faced with such high debt hurdles to overcome that it is unlikely many of them could survive for an extended period of time. It is unknown how wide-spread this dividend model has become and how large and wide-ranging the various fees are these days, but it is known that there are lots of questionable activities going on, and it is also known that the regulatory bodies have little authority to appropriately monitor these activities. As is usually the case, there will be lots of intervention following a broad meltdown which hurts the financial industry, or when large investor classes are harmed by portfolio companies which are ultimately brought public.

As more investors become aware of these shenanigans, the bond market is likely to experience a troubling effect. As an increasing number of big-moneyed PEF's seek out larger firms as targets, the bond market could become destabilized. Imagine what might occur after a few large-cap companies are taken over by PEF's. Suddenly great amounts of debt might be put on the balance sheets of previously conservatively run companies. Following completion of a few of these types of large-scale deals, bond investors would get nervous and demand much greater premiums on investments for all companies issuing bonds. Such demands would have the net effect of driving up interest rates for all issuers of debt. The US government would not be exempt, and would be forced to raise the rates paid to investors for government securities. This could turn out very nicely for investors who choose only to invest in US government securities, but would not turn out so well for investors in the corporate bond market and the equity markets, as less stable companies would see investors rush for the exits. This is not all that different than what occurred in the late 1980's when the US experienced a large number of leveraged buyouts, which I suppose is to be expected, since everything is cyclical.

Pro Forma and GAAP

The percentage of companies which choose to report pro forma numbers rather than reporting under GAAP (Generally Accepted Accounting Principles) ebbs and flows in peaks and valleys, along with the economic cycle. Talk is that the market may have entered the cycle phase in which more companies choose pro forma over GAAP. There could be many reasons for such a cycle's existence. One is that when business conditions are very good, a greater percentage of companies can report under GAAP because they generally have less to hide. When the climate starts to deteriorate, however, more companies tend to start using pro forma, as it gives them more of an ability to massage their numbers so that investors will see what company management would prefer that they see. Another reason is that following stock market downturns, public ire is raised and regulators come out of their hiding places to impose greater penalties on those who deal in fuzzy figures. This has the effect of driving more companies to GAAP, as they begin to believe that massaging their numbers may not be worth the risk to their reputations and personal fortunes. Whatever the reason, 2005 appears to have marked the turnaround towards pro forma once again. Since the regulators have been pounding away for a few years now, I am inclined to believe that the recent resurgence in pro forma statements has more to do with the need to massage numbers to make those numbers appear better, and less to do with regulatory issues.

Retailers and restaurants have been using it for years, and many have come under scrutiny and been forced to change their financial reporting by the FASB (Financial Accounting Standards Board). Other industry sectors are using it as well. The "it" I am referring to is lease accounting, which can make reading a financial statement akin to watching a magic show. This, along with pension, retiree health insurance, and hedge accounting are coming under increasing scrutiny while partial solutions for options expensing are being implemented. Hopefully with all the scrutiny, soon pro forma and GAAP will come into a tighter range on a permanent basis, but until this happens, beware. The difference between to two can be a leading indicator of a significant stock market correction to come.

Speaking of options expensing, evidence is starting to accumulate that at least several public companies' boards have been engaging in the practice of backdating options awards to executives. This is a practice where the effective date of the award plan is set on the date the stock hit a low point during a given period. This allows the recipient of the options award to achieve an ultimate gain that would be greater than otherwise achieved, in some cases very significantly. There will be a lot more information concerning this practice in the news in the ensuing years, but for now, be aware that it exists and that returns may be affected by it.

All of these accounting issues are brought to the reader's attention because they can have an effect on an individual security, on an industry sector, and/or on an entire market. Any regulatory changes affecting reporting requirements can have potentially large effects, and investors must be aware that changes are occurring concerning some of these issues and are likely to occur for the others.

Reported Versus Operating Earnings

Accounting maneuvers have always been used en masse by public companies. During periods when some companies are being more aggressive than usual without repercussions from regulatory bodies, other companies join in so that they can keep up the appearance of remaining competitive in reporting their numbers. The stock market recently came off a period (the bubble) in which the difference between reported and operating earnings so grossly affected price earnings ratios that the ratios calculated using each set of numbers could vary by almost 100%!

The "operating" in operating earnings generally excludes "extraordinary" and other items. The trouble is, however, that many companies become addicted to reporting operating earnings as they go from year-to-year writing off huge chunks of capital as their balance sheets deteriorate. I have found over the years that a good indication of when the stock market has reached the bottom of a cycle, P/E's calculated using reported and operating earnings are equal. This seems to have occurred following the crash in 1987 and briefly on another occasion since then. Strangely, they never came together following the recent stock market crash. That has left me very skeptical of the recovery of the last few years. I find that when the difference between the two measurements gets to about 25%, it's nature's little way of suggesting an approaching market stall or correction.

Studies have been conducted which show a marked divergence between the profits reported to the Internal Revenue Service and those reported to company shareholders. By some measures, recent divergence has climbed to levels similar to those which existed at the height of the 1999/2000 bubble in percentage terms. Should the companies experience similar profits corrections to that which they experienced beginning in 2000, it is virtually guaranteed that the stock market would suffer a serious correction.

US, Inc.

By the late 1990's, the US financial markets had come to a place that resembled Japan, Inc. of the late 1980's. Most Japanese companies had stakes in each other at that point. This meant that financial firms controlled manufacturing firms, manufacturing firms controlled financial firms, usually with a few firms together controlling the fate of another firm, and that firm having a stake in yet another company. This crossover of ownership caused the companies to engage in all sorts of behavior which might not have occurred had all the companies maintained true independence. Eventually, when the stock and real estate markets began to unwind, all companies' share prices fell together because they all owned stakes in each other. The end result was that the Japanese market would fall by some 80% over 13 years.

US investors have entrusted their stock investing to financial institutions (pension funds, mutual funds, etc.) whose interests are often closely tied to the management of the companies they are investing in. And their money under management has been growing exponentially. With this growth, financially oriented companies are wielding more influence than ever before, and that influence is growing. The business of money has become so desirable a business to be in, that estimates are that as much as one-half of S&P500 earnings only a few years ago were attributed to the combination of companies in the finance industries and the finance arms of companies in other industries. America's 100 largest money mangers today hold well over half of all US stocks. Many of these companies are public or are owned by other public companies. They could be financial arms of diversified companies or financial components of multi-pronged financial firms. Either way, they have many conflicts of interest, not that different then what has been brought out by Eliot Spitzer's investigations.

Depending on whom one listens to, estimates put the share of stocks held by individual investors in the US at less than 30%, down considerably from prior periods. This may be attributed to the most recent market plunge which "evaporated" much of individual investors' holdings, but also may be due to many investors' moves into real estate (the next "evaporation"). Another reason is that over the years, investors have been persuaded that they cannot do better than the money managers, and they are increasingly handing over assets to money management firms. Strangely, when this type of exchange occurs en masse, it could be a sign of big problems to come, for many of the reasons discussed throughout this book.

It makes some sense that in the post-industrial US society envisioned by many that a point may soon be reached where almost all profits are derived from financial activities and other services, as most manufacturing finds its way to emerging markets where manufacturers compete with one another to earn as little as a penny on the dollar.

Corporations have taken a break from branching out into unrelated areas such as entertainment companies and professional sports teams. But I'm sure it's only a matter of time before they resume their shopping spree, which reminds me of one of my favorite futuristic movies from the 1970's. You've probably guessed it already. The movie is *Rollerball*, starring James Caan. The setting is the future, where city-corporations such as New York, Houston, and Tokyo control the world, battles are waged in the roller rink, and the individual spirit is suppressed in the name of the corporation, as its executives (who fantasize about being "roller-ballers") control everything from behind the scenes.

Empires

General Electric (GE) is widely considered the master of empire building and empire management. Under Jack Welch, the company became determined to create, maintain and/or purchase a number one or two position in every industry in which it decided to compete. The customer wants quality, and when a company can show that its goods and services are the best, that company's reputation and value soars. This strategy paid off handsomely in the 1980's and 1990's, along with all the cost cutting moves by the conglomerate. Under Jeffrey Immelt, the company is remaking itself once again, moving more into health-related products and services, and exiting certain financial oriented businesses. Its shear size and reputation allows it a degree of freedom not enjoyed by many other companies. Although its stock had lost two-thirds of its value in the recent stock market crash, shareholders can rest assured that the stock will not go to zero in our lifetimes.

Other companies have attempted to mirror GE's moves. Unfortunately for them, if their targets were so valuable, it's likely GE or Berkshire Hathaway or United Technologies would have gotten there first. So the end result is conglomerates like Tyco and Cendant, with overpaid emperors. Typically what happens is that the emperor understands that the bigger he can make his company, the more he can justify an ever-increasing compensation package for himself. Generally his company takes on more debt in doing so, but why should the emperor be concerned about this debt? With some luck, he will grow the company for 20 years, amass a fortune, and when he retires, the debt and problems will be left for somebody else to deal with. Ah, if only it always worked out that way.

Each of these companies reached the inflection point and came to the realization that instead of acquiring more divisions, they would be better off splitting their empires into pieces. But here's the really tricky part. When the emperors were building these empires, the rationale for an increasing stock price was that the pieces of the empire were more valuable together than they were alone. Now the rationale is that the pieces are more valuable alone than they are together. What's going on here? These concepts are complete polar opposites! Sadly, what this becomes is an interesting study on hope in the minds of investors, as their money is taken away from them.

So who typically benefits in these types of situations? Clearly the investment banks and Wall Street law firms do quite well for themselves. They each earn huge fees building these empires up and then again tearing them down. And the executives of the empires make out very nicely (provided they don't get into legal trouble), as they bring in allied board members who give a pass on outsized compensation packages to the detriment of shareholders and many employees. Of course, savvy traders do very nicely for themselves, as they see the situation for what it is long before the majority of market participants.

Mutual Fund Cash Positions

The percentage of cash held by mutual funds in relation to their total assets under management has been a reliable gage of the health of the stock market for many decades. My studies indicate that local stock market lows are reached when mutual fund cash position in aggregate reaches highs exceeding 9%. Strangely, at the low point of the 2000-2003 bear market, the aggregate mutual fund cash position saw a high of only about 6%. Cash levels have since fallen to around half that level, which has not been seen since the early 1970's. These events could be signaling that stock market and cash position patterns of the 1970's and 80's will return. Should such a scenario unfold, the stock market may not bottom until cash positions reach 9% to 11%. Having seen earlier that mutual funds and other financial institutions control a much larger percentage of money in the stock market than they had in the past, it is all the more important to keep a close watch of these figures, as those entities will have even more impact on the market than they had in the past.

Cycles

There are many cycles which savvy traders and investors utilize when making investment decisions. These cycles have been written about and discussed so much over the years that they are more or less considered common knowledge in the industry. A few of the currently meaningful ones are coming up and should be noted. First is the 80-week cycle of "local" lows, due to make its next visit in the spring of 2006. Second is the presidential cycle which suggests that 2006 is due to be the worst year of the four-year presidential cycle. Third is the statistic that a year ending in the digit "6" tends to be a weaker year in terms of total stock market returns. These are the negatives. However, on the positive side, the Nasdaq has been retracing the pattern of the Dow of the 1930's, and if history is a guide, the Nasdaq could move up nearly 100% from its October, 2005 lows. Assuming the Nasdaq continues to follow this pattern, it could rise through 2007 before falling by 50%. Which scenario unfolds will be determined by prevailing market forces, and it is essential to monitor those forces on a continuous basis in order to out-perform the markets.

There are numerous other cycles which the pros use to their advantage, at the small investor's expense, and of course there is no way of knowing which of any cycles or patterns will repeat themselves. The small investor must be aware that the pros have a multitude of information at their fingertips, and if that investor doesn't have the same information immediately available, then he/she is not playing the game with a full deck.

3

FOR THE NOVICE

The Greatest Bubbles

Asset bubbles have been around since mankind began valuing anything desired by consumers. In the earliest days this might have been the remains from the last kill or the stash of nuts going into the long, cold winter. Those who were savvy enough to collect and store the desired goods were able to name their price when it came time to sell. As winter was in full swing, I am certain there was a very high price to pay for the best food, clothing, shelter, and whatever "luxury" items might have existed at the time. Moving fast forward to the Dutch tulip bulb mania of the 1630's, observers recorded a 60-fold rise in price over a two-year period, followed by a fall that brought that price down to a fraction of its original starting point in just a few short months, reminiscent of many internet stocks in the modern equivalent of the tulip bulb mania (refer to the book cover for a typical bubble pattern). The Dow exhibited similar behavior in the 1920's with about a six-fold increase in ten years, followed by a three-year plunge to a value which was one-half its starting point from the early 20's (compare this with its twelve-fold increase from the early 1980's through 2000). Other fine examples include Japan's Nikkei which saw about a ten-fold increase from 1974 through 1989, and the Nasdaq's approximate 16-fold increase from 1990 to 2000! The 1990's and early 2000's saw emerging and developed markets undergo enormous corrections at varying times during various crises. One cannot even be sure if many of these corrections have run their course.

The interesting thing about bubbles is that until recently, they occurred only about once per generation. A likely reason for this had been that once badly burned by a bubble, an entire generation of investors swore off investing, and the necessary public interest to fuel a new bubble was not available until a new generation of fools, with little memory of the pain caused by the previous bubble, came along.

What is so interesting now is that there have been many bubbles recently in a very short period of time. Japan got hit in 1990, and just about every stock market had taken a hit at some point from the mid-1990's through 2003. And the world is currently getting ready for the popping of a world-wide real estate bubble. Never before have there been so many bubbles in such a short period of time combined with investors' willingness to stay the course and keep investing. Perhaps investors have simply come to terms with the knowledge that there will always be bubbles, and they are no longer as fazed by them as were previous generations of investors. Or perhaps investors are only impacted following the one-two punch of a stock market crash and a real estate market crash together. I guess the answers will present themselves in the ensuing years.

Brokers' Oldest Tricks

Whether it was the stock broker in the 1980's or 1990's, or it's the stock pickers on cable television (TV) today, the game is similar. A technique used by many brokers was to call a list of clients or potential clients and talk up a stock. Then they might call people from a second list and talk down the same stock. If the stock went up, they could call people on the first list and boast of their stock-picking prowess. If they could not get a person on that list as a client, they might repeat the technique again with the same stock or with a different stock. If the brokers were correct with their predictions the second time, their track records looked great. This time, the brokers probably got a new client. Likewise, if the stock went down, the brokers had their list of people to call. With either scenario, after a few successful calls the brokers would look like geniuses.

The stock pickers on television function in a similar manner. They pick a stock they believe may go up. If the stock goes down, they usually try their best never to mention it again. If the stock goes up, however, viewers will likely hear them touting their stock-picking prowess over and over. The reality is that if these people were so good at picking stocks, would they really be wasting their time calling strangers on the telephone? Or would they really be wasting their time on TV when they could be back at their offices figuring out their next moves? The answer is no to both of these questions. The majority of brokers, advisors, and money managers make their money from fees which they charge their clients, not from their picks. And the reality is that most of the TV people are entertainers, not successful stock pickers.

Stock Market Indexes

It is very important to remember that stock indexes are created by people. And almost all things created by people can be controlled by people. This means that indexes can be manipulated. Few people think about this concept, but many have been burned by it. There is a common belief that investors in Dow stocks will be relatively safe and will prosper. Unfortunately, this may not be true for long periods of time, as in the period from 1929 to the early 1950's when the Dow went nowhere for 24 years. But there is something far more sinister out there. Some investors do not purchase the Dow index, but rather, several of the individual stocks which comprise the Dow. While the Dow itself may be a fantastic investment over a 20- or 30-year period, there could be several Dow stocks which go nowhere during a Dow run. General Motors is an example of a Dow stock hovering around 20-year lows. But far worse, think of one-time star performer, Bethlehem Steel, which while dying a slow death, was removed from the Dow and put out to pasture. Investors who were lucky enough to get out while it was still in the Dow did far better than those who rode it into oblivion.

The point is that the powers that be are able to decide at any time that they are unhappy with the stocks in the Dow, and embark on a reshuffling to create a portfolio of stocks in the Dow which are more "representative" of the makeup of the US economy at a given time. Recently (2004), American International Group, Pfizer, and Verizon replaced AT&T, Kodak, and International Paper in the Dow. In 1999, four new stocks were moved in to replace four older stocks. This is a reshuffling of seven out of thirty stocks in a five-year period. That works out to a 23% change in the makeup of the Dow in only five years! Lucent is still one of the most widely held stocks for no other reason than it was a spin-off of AT&T (then a Dow stock) and advisors recommended that their clients hold onto it for the long term. Many former Dow stocks have gone out of business or were absorbed into other companies, so it is difficult to know how the original Dow might have performed over the last century, but one can be certain that it is not nearly as well as the recorded numbers for the Dow. In recent years, the Nasdaq has seen tremendous turnover of its component stocks as well. I can only wonder what the level of the Nasdaq would be today had all its components been frozen in place in early March of 2000.

There are a couple of major things to take away from all this information. The first is obvious. A passive investor is better off buying indexes than trying to pick stocks (unless that investor has some real advantage in evaluating a particular stock). Second, nobody should believe the pros when they say stocks go up over time, because this is an inaccurate statement. Indexes go up over time because their component stocks are selected by people, and selection of stocks for the indexes is governed by one rule…. survival of the fittest.

New-Old Games on Wall Street

There are increasing reports that many brokerage firms and banks with brokerage units are keeping customer money in low-yielding cash accounts rather than their higher-yielding money-market fund counterparts. One large discount broker happily kept customers in an account earning less than 1%, even while it had money-market funds yielding close to 4%. This may not seem like a big difference at first glance, but if an investor has $100,000 sitting in the lower yielding account, the difference in interest would be about $1000 versus $4000 over the course of a year, which is fairly significant, and, in fact, is a difference of 300%! This is one of the reasons this firm was able to report such increased earnings in recent years. And there are plenty of firms doing this. Why shouldn't this money go into the account holder's pocket instead of going into the pockets of brokerage firm shareholders and executives? Why don't more investors watch these things more closely? Why isn't the Fed or another government agency warning the small investor to watch more closely? The most important question an investor should be asking is why he/she should trust these firms or anyone else to look out for his/her best interest (pardon the pun).

A popular trick used by the banks and brokerages is the promotion. One might offer an investor three months of attractive interest rates if that investor brings in $25,000 or $50,000. At the end of the three months, the investor may forget to monitor the account, and when he/she opens a statement six months later, only then recalls that the high interest rate had expired three months earlier. Unfortunately, for the last three months that investor had been getting a rate that was even lower than the rate he/she was getting before bringing the new money to the firm. By this time, the investor has likely ended up with a lower total return than had he/she initially done nothing.

If these financial institutions that are entrusted with our money are able to do this with the most simple of investments (yields on savings and money-market accounts), just think of what is probably going on in all the other more complicated areas (think mortgages, stocks, options, etc.). There is a very high likelihood that in these other areas the investor is getting completely taken to the cleaners. What should be taken away from all this is that an investor must monitor interest rates in all their savings accounts very closely every month, and always seek out the highest returns from the safest products.

Wal-Mart

Wal-Mart has done a lot of great things for the US. Wal-Mart has also done a few things that turned out to be not so great for the US. As it turns out, there is no hugely successful company that has only done good. So why has Wal-Mart become so politically incorrect? Could it be because all the other retailers are banding together to target Wal-Mart in every way they can, much as what occurred with Microsoft? Could it be that many owners of small businesses have been put out of business or risk being put out of business by Wal-Mart? I believe it is for these and many other reasons. But perhaps the biggest reason is likely to surprise many people.

One of the most profitable businesses in the US is the business of money, and one area of the business of money is the traditional business of banking. Banks essentially hold onto peoples' cash for a fee (interest) and use that cash to generate higher returns for themselves. Wal-Mart has announced that it wishes to get into the banking business. In so doing, it would immediately lower banking costs to most of its customers, who are generally gouged by the banks. In a short time, Wal-Mart could become an extremely formidable competitor in the money business. Just imagine how Wal-Mart could shake up this business as it did all the others it entered. It could bring low fee (or no fee) checking and credit card accounts to its customers, and maybe even lower-cost mortgages and insurance. If Wal-Mart could enter these businesses, it could expect unlimited growth.

Just a few short years ago, S&P500 companies engaged in finance-related activities were generating about 50% of total index profits. Even in early 2006, with the yield curve inverting, they were still generating about 25% of the index's profits. It is very clear to me that these businesses have a very strong incentive to keep giant, efficient companies like Wal-Mart, with hundreds of millions of customers out of the business of money. I am not implying that companies in the money business are conspiring to keep Wal-Mart down, but I can certainly see why they would want to do so. If Wal-Mart were given free reign to compete, and others could follow, the money industry could potentially lose half its revenues and profits in a ten-year period.

The Truth about Mutual Funds

Numerous articles from newspapers, books, and countless other sources have shown over and over that the average mutual fund as well as the average hedge fund underperforms the stock market indexes over an extended period of time. Strong arguments have been made to show that the typical mutual fund investor makes close to nothing on his/her investments, and far worse after taxes and inflation. The generally accepted reason for this underperformance is that the small investor chases performance, and as the typical mutual fund is trying to get investors' money, the fund family heavily markets its best performing funds. Naturally, the small investor invests in those funds. Since everything is cyclical, after the small investor gets into those high performing funds, their returns go negative. Following a bad year or two, the investor sells the funds. In the meantime, another sector has started performing well, and of course, the small investor does not participate until he/she sees outstanding results. Again, of course, as before, the small investor is too late to the game. I'm not going to spend time rehashing any more of this information, but rather, conclude that it is already common knowledge, and use it as a foundation on which to discuss what it all means.

Year-end is a particularly treacherous time to be a mutual fund investor, as this is the time period in which funds with gains declare capital gains taxes, and pass them on to their shareholders. A wise investor will generally purchase a fund immediately following a large distribution, hold the fund for nearly a year of gains, and then sell just before the effective date of capital gains distribution, or simply hold that fund in a non-taxable account. The novice investor will typically see that a fund has performed well, buy the fund without thinking about who might be responsible for the taxes, and find out when he/she receives a 1099 from the fund that a large tax bill on gains is owed to the government. This is one of the grandest Ponzi schemes in the financial markets. While the novice investor who is new to the fund pays all the taxes, the seasoned investor who reaped the benefits of the gains throughout the year walks away without the burden of the fund's tax bill, and only has his own tax bill to consider.

Any time a fund has a big year, an investor must consider tax consequences. Likewise, when a fund has had a couple of good years following a couple of bad years, the investor should take extra precaution. This is because the fund may not have owed taxes in its first up year because it had tax-loss carryovers from the prior poor years. However, by the time the fund gets to the second year of solid performance, it may have used up its tax credits. In such a case, the shareholders in the fund when the fund declares its gains distributions at year-end will bear the burden of those taxes. It is virtually nonexistent for a fund company representative to warn an investor of these things when called on the phone, unless the investor specifically requests such information. The investor is almost always responsible for inquiring or doing his/her own research on these matters.

But wait, it gets worse. The worst part of all is that the average fund underperforms its index equivalent. Once taxes are included in the calculation, after-tax performance drops even more (the exact numbers vary, but some estimates are as much as 2 or 3% below index performance, on average). Nobody knows the exact number, as the poorest performing funds are continuously being closed or merged with strong performers, and their performance records are no longer included in the averages. For all these reasons, it is generally safest to go with the lowest-cost index fund at a well-known mutual fund company, if one wishes to be in a mutual fund.

Do It Yourself

A friend called me and asked if she should buy a couple of particular stocks. We talked about the pluses and minuses of each potential purchase, and potential outcomes under different scenarios. I explained that based on historical numbers, most stocks were fairly valued to overvalued at that time, and that there was a lot of risk in the market in general. I then went on to explain to her that she would be competing against people who invest full time, and who have been doing it for their entire careers. When I could see that she still didn't understand what I was implying, I went on to explain that she should imagine a trader from Wall Street suddenly being asked to compete against her in her line of work. She laughed and made it very clear to me that she now understood my message. That message is that unless an investor is willing to invest a lot of time following the stock market, the economy, the industry of the stock (or sector) she plans to buy, and the company of that stock, or unless she is an expert in that industry, she probably should not be an active investor. She more than likely is best off in a well run low-cost index fund.

Mafia

In the 1990's, it was widely reported that the mafia had joined the movement of "legitimate" businesspeople into the "chop shops" (also known as "boiler rooms"), and began manipulating stocks to the detriment of their "clients". If this was true, can you blame them? For someone without a conscience and with a good legal team, the potential gains far outweighed the risks. And the work wasn't the least bit dangerous!

Regulators got wind of what was going on and cracked down on this to a large extent. But what they accomplished was that they chased the rooster out of the henhouse and let the wolf in. The wolf here is the large, established, "reputable" Wall Street firm. When the chop shop brokers called us on the phone and tried to get us to invest, we knew to be wary because we had never heard of them, but when Wall Street reached out to us on CNBC, and in the papers, magazines and Saturday talk shows in the late 1990's, we trusted them. After all, the authorities were watching out for us, as they had just driven most of the chop shops out of business, and there were only legitimate players left.

Well, as it turned out, the enemy you trust is the worst type of foe you can possibly have, precisely because you trust him.

Ranking the Experts

Many publications put out annual rankings of research firms which are based on accuracy of predictions across a broad spectrum of industry sectors. Results in recent years have been surprising. Generally, one would expect that the larger, brand-name Wall Street firms would be among the most highly ranked, but this has not been the case. The firms appearing at the top of these lists have tended to be smaller, far less known firms, and there has generally been considerable distance between these firms and the larger ones. I leave the reader to draw his/her own conclusions.

One interesting question I raise is that if the large Wall Street firms' proprietary trading units are making so much money, they have to be right a lot more often than they are wrong. But if this is the case, then how can their research arms be so far off? Is it possible that even after all the disclosed conflicts of interest on Wall Street, that firms' researchers are giving opinions to win banking business at the expense of their clients? After all, how can we reconcile the difference in performance between their research groups and their proprietary trading units?

Cramer, *Mad Money*, and the Rest of Them

Whether it's Jim Cramer (Cramer) or someone else the investor is "tuned in to" for advice, there are certain things to be aware of. Let's analyze what Cramer's TV show, *Mad Money* is all about.

One of Cramer's favorite sayings for an entire year was that Alan Greenspan (Greenspan) should be at Sunrise Senior Living. What I believe Cramer really meant to say was that he was angry that Greenspan popped the technology bubble a few years ago, and in doing so, probably caused Cramer to lose some business. Cramer believes that Greenspan should not have raised interest rates as high as he did in 2000, and was upset that Greenspan was doing it again in 2005. In reality, however, Greenspan should probably have started raising rates much earlier and more rapidly than he did in both cases, and that likely would have prevented the 2000 bubble in the first place, as it might have prevented the current stock market echo bubble, real estate bubble, and inflation situation. Cramer's goal is to make money, and that means making money today, likely at the expense of tomorrow. Why else would he be so upset at the Fed for trying to do its job by tempering the economy. If anything, Cramer should be thanking Greenspan for helping him out so many times.

Nobody has more of a right to be upset with Greenspan than I do, but I'm upset for a different reason than Cramer. I blame Greenspan for allowing the 1990's stock market bubble to form in the first place. I also hold Greenspan responsible for allowing the current housing bubble to form, as he kept interest rates ridiculously low for so long while lending standards completely deteriorated. Further, Greenspan's housing bubble has helped create what I refer to as our "real inflation" situation. Having erred in the 1990's, I don't think Greenspan wanted things to get quite as out of hand this time around. He also had to consider the transition to Ben Bernanke (Bernanke) as the new Fed head. Had Greenspan not been raising rates for over 18 months, Bernanke would have been forced to enact massive interest rate increases to deal with the inflation situation which Greenspan is responsible for creating. Greenspan did a great job of putting off dealing with the inevitable and has passed the heavy lifting on to poor Ben Bernanke (in fairness, of course, Greenspan wasn't dealt the greatest hand either when he took over the reigns at the Fed 19 years earlier).

Cramer touts himself as a master stock picker, but I beg to differ. In early 2005, Cramer spent a lot of time talking about General Motors on his show, *Mad Money*. He hated GM at 25, saying it would go much lower, then loved it at 33 after Kirk Kerkorian got in, hated it again at 31, and liked it again at 35 after the unions said they would talk. For a couple of months, he was always chasing it and always seemed to be going in the wrong direction. If Cramer really understood the market so well, wouldn't he have figured out that given all the easy money floating around and all the hedge funds and private-equity funds awash in cash, some player would have come in even if Kerkorian had not? I realized this, and got in for a quick trade. Who knows? Maybe in the long run Cramer will turn out to be right now that he finally made up his mind that the stock will go down. But if he is the great trader he claims to be, wouldn't he have traded this stock on the right side several times in 2005, and made a bundle doing so? GM's price has fluctuated roughly 30% up and down several times over the course of the year and Cramer was never able to catch it.

Cramer has made lots of great calls (and actually gives his listeners some really useful information provided this information is used on their own terms), but he has also made plenty of bad ones. I laughed every day while he trashed Netflix as its stock price crept along at 9 or 10, claiming the company was finished. But why would this company be finished? They were gaining market share rapidly, had no real competitors, and an ever-increasing percentage of movie companies' profits continued to come from rentals and sales of DVD's. Netflix had one of the best franchises an investor could find, and at its low, its price-to-sales ratio was only one, less than the average stock at that time, and it had virtually no debt! For all we know, Cramer never even really analyzed this company. He may just have a couple of friends who told him the stock is a dog, and in doing so were relying on Cramer to drive the share price down so they could reap a fortune being short the stock.

I am not trying to bash Cramer. What I am trying to convey is that even a guy like Cramer (who I believe genuinely wants to help the small investor) makes lots of mistakes and has lots of self-interests which may cause him to issue "buys" and "sells" for the wrong reasons. And if he is susceptible to this, then virtually any-one in the business is. The bottom line is that an investor should take everything she is told with a grain of salt, do her own research, and only buy and sell that which she understands very well (because there are lots of people out there who understand each and every company a lot better than she does, and they are trad-ing against her).

I really want to reinforce my overall message, so I have to stay with the Cramer subject. For much of the earlier part of 2005, Cramer touted the stock of his long-time friend (Eddie Lampert), Sears Holdings (Sears), and simultaneously trashed Wal-Mart.

Hmmmm … Is this a co-incidence?

Doesn't Sears stand to benefit greatly if Cramer is telling everyone to sell Wal-Mart while recommending they buy Sears? He did fully disclose his personal rela-tionship with Lampert, and in doing so, he has come clean to viewers, but I per-sonally believe this is one set of stocks he should have stayed far away from.

Cramer has sited unnamed "sources" and contacts for his information on various stocks. This is an area which demands some attention. Did anyone think that Cramer's sources and contacts might be "playing" him? His sources could very well sell into his "buy" recommendations and buy into his "sell" recommendations. And there would be nothing illegal about this. When Cramer talks to his sources for their opinions on a stock or an industry he may not even know if they are "long" or "short", or if they have friends who are. This information he is so privy to could be garbage, or even worse. It may be the reverse of what an investor truly needs to know. The bottom line is that Cramer is an entertainer, and often not a guy to take seriously, although there are times when he tells things as they are, like when he was doing the Harvard road show in early 2006. On that show he admitted that the investing business is half luck. And it is.

One thing anyone who tunes into Cramer's show must remember is that it is not about making money. It is about gambling with money, hence *Mad Money*. When people call into his show and ask about buying QQQQ or SPY or DIA, he generally refuses their calls. He does this because if he told callers to buy these ETF's, he might have a boring show (which might be pulled from the air), and two of his goals are to get people to do more trading of individual stocks and to become addicted to his show. This, in turn, boosts the show's ratings for General Electric, helps him sell more books, and helps his company TheStreet.com attract more internet viewers. None of these things are necessarily in an investor's best interests, but rather, in the end, serve the interests of others. The net effect is that he has a more entertaining show, and as a result, gets to stay on the air three times per night, gets paid a lot more from NBC, gets to promote his book so that he makes more money, and the people who may be playing him get to make lots of money off of the viewers who blindly follow Cramer's instructions.

Cramer is a true market seer. Who else was pounding the table to buy technology in February, 2000, and then by mid-March sold everything (Cramer's revelation on *Mad Money*, 12/27/05)? Recognize of course that this can mean lots of things. Assuming that he really sold everything, how does one go from being a complete bull to a complete bear in one month? Is it possible he was really a bear in February, but held himself out as a bull so that he could get out at the top? Is this shrewd trading, legal market manipulation, did Cramer simply read the Barron's article which foretold of the coming crash, or is it a combination of all these things? I don't know the answers, but these are all questions that should be asked if someone is going to follow his advice. And what does all this mean for today's investor who watches his show, and buys on his recommendations? How will these investors be affected if Cramer suddenly changes his mind one day and announces that he is no longer a bull, and is in fact a bear? And how will these investors feel if it later comes out that Cramer sold many of his investments before telling his viewers it was time to sell? Again, these are all questions that viewers of his show or any other show need to ask themselves over and over again before acting on advice.

For all his shortcomings, Cramer can be very informative. Several times a week he will share some valuable information with his audience which can be used later to either make some money or avoid losing some money. One of his studies looked at a number of publicly traded mutual fund companies and compared the results of the stock market return of shares in those mutual fund companies themselves to the returns of each company's best performing diversified fund over a period of years. He found that in each case, the fund company shares outperformed the best fund that it managed. The conclusion he reached is that managing money is a great business, and that investors should own shares of the fund companies rather than giving them more money to manage. I guess this is why everyone in the industry wants to own a mutual fund or a hedge fund. These vehicles are set up to create winners and losers. The winners are the owners, managers, and employees of the funds. The losers are the least savvy investors in the funds.

I need to stress a final time that for all the Cramer bashing I have done I still believe that Cramer is one of the best in the business. I singled out his show in an effort to convey that if someone this good has vulnerabilities, then the investor had better watch out for everyone else! I am only pointing out these issues so that the trusting, small, unsophisticated investor is not taken advantage of. Since so many viewers watch Cramer's show, it serves as an outstanding teaching tool to illustrate many of the points I have made throughout this book, so I thank Cramer for putting himself out there the way he does.

I try to catch part of Cramer's show most nights for many reasons. As I stated before, he can disseminate some very useful information, provided this information is properly utilized. He also has the power to move the market, which nobody should ignore. He has made some big blunders (many of which I have not discussed) but overall, he happened to have an excellent track record in 2005. Whether he will continue to do well, however, is another issue, especially if the market falls in 2006.

Wall Street Compensation Revisited

Wall Street's average compensation increase in 2005 over 2004 was about 15%, with bonuses for 2005 coming in at about a cool $21.5 billion, a new record. This is even greater than at the end of the raging bull market of the 1990's! Estimates are that this startling sum translates into something on the order of an average of $1 million for a typical trader at a major firm, and well over $125,000 per employee, on top of base salaries.

The stock market indexes essentially broke even for the year in real terms, and the typical investor made no money in 2005.

As Mel Brooks once said, "It's good to be the king."

4

REAL ESTATE

Housing Boom?

Talk of a housing boom that could run forever appears to have been toned down a bit lately. Anyone who doubts that the real estate market is on a precipice ought to consider the following information very carefully. There are increasing reports that major mortgage lenders have been making it more difficult for borrowers to qualify for adjustable-rate mortgages. Prior to the combination of increasing interest rates, jaw-boning by the Fed, and a realization that the top of the real estate market may have been reached, these and other types of more exotic mortgages were about as easy to get as opening a bank account. With home ownership rates in the US at all-time highs, tightening of lending standards has already had an effect on the real estate market.

For those who refuse to believe the real estate market is falling to earth, one needs only look to Australia for guidance. Following many years of double-digit returns, the major markets of Sydney and Melbourne have finally taken some hits. Whether Australia's market stalls or goes into a downturn is unclear at this point, but a warning flag has been raised for the rest of the world.

Easy Money and Interest Rates

Many forces were responsible for driving the real estate bubble, but among the most notable was the availability of easy money. The Fed held rates at levels below the real rate of inflation for an extended period of time as the Bank of Japan held rates effectively at zero. Even after the Fed raised rates to bring the 10-year US Treasury to 4% by mid-2005 versus only about 3% and 1.5% for German and Japanese equivalents, respectively, money was still cheap, even cheaper in real terms, and cheaper still when accounting for "stealth" inflation.

At that time, to attract investors, Fannie Mae and Freddie Mac were offering yields of about 5.5%, and sub-prime mortgage securities were yielding multiples of Treasuries. Institutions (including many foreign ones) were drawn to the higher yields of the various mortgage securities, especially those guaranteed by government-sponsored entities like Fannie and Freddie, which enabled lenders to keep lending. But the rates which sub-prime securities were paying were a clear red flag. Did it really make sense that they could afford to pay such high rates of return when the competition was so much lower? Whenever such a huge disparity exists, it exists for a reason. In this case it was the indicator of instability, as investors demanded significantly higher interest rates to compensate them for the risks involved. It is the market's natural way of communicating that there is a problem.

Home-Construction Index

Figures for any national home construction index in the US will show about a 1000% increase from 2000 to 2005. And as we have seen before with stock markets, a curve tracing home-construction index data on a graph reveals a classic bubble pattern. It is very clear to me that the bubble had popped in 2005, or will do so in 2006 at the latest. The ensuing correction might not be of the recent 80% magnitude experienced by the Nasdaq, but it will nevertheless be considerable.

New Homes

The US went from about 1.2 million new homes started in 1995 to almost double that amount in 2005. A curve traced by the annual data plotted on a graph reveals the appearance of a classic bubble pattern. Taken together with the percentage of home ownership (nearing 70% of households, an all-time high), the rate of increase in population and many other factors, if the bubble did not pop in 2005, it will certainly do so in 2006.

Whether referring to the price of condo's and co-op's, or to the price of houses, curves fitting the data all yield hyperbolic-type patterns. All these curves are sending clear messages that the boom is unsustainable, and is therefore over. These classic chart patterns suggest that the real estate boom will end either with a crash or with a major cool down. Either of these scenarios can mean disaster for many people who bought in the years immediately preceding the peak. A crash, however, can still cause great harm to people who bought several years prior, if they bought in one of the bubble markets and/or if their finances were not what they should have been.

Risky Loans

The Federal Housing Agency had moved away from making risky loans, accounting for a low single-digit percentage of such loans by 2005. At the same time, subprime lenders stepped up to the plate, and saw exponential growth in their mortgage portfolios. In addition, interest-only loans as a percentage of new mortgages in the subprime market rose from virtually nothing to well over 25% in just a few years. More recently, "low-doc" and "no-doc" loans (low documentation and no documentation of finances), and their relatives, NINA's (no income, no assets) had been taking over the mortgage loan scene. Reports are that the percentage of low doc, no doc loans had been rising rapidly through 2006 and could account for as much as half of subprime loans. By early 2006, total US mortgage-backed debt had purportedly surpassed total US Treasury debt, and investors world-wide were buying much of this mortgage debt. A familiar equivalent would be investing in high-yield debt, or "junk" bonds.

This information is alarming, because entities not sponsored by the government had been gaining market share very rapidly, and without any quasi-backing from the government, they are on their own. If things go bad and their lenders want their money back, these entities could collapse. When the market turns, these subprime lenders will have a tough time collecting their money, but will still have to meet their obligations to their investors. They will be forced to take possession of properties belonging to borrowers who default, and they will place those properties on the market for resale to raise cash. Such actions will put more home inventory on the market and cause prices to fall. This could send the market into a vicious downward cycle in which prices fall further and further until they reach some equilibrium level. The extension of such easy credit is not unlike what went on during the recent stock market bubble when high-tech companies were selling much of their product on credit to other businesses, and we all know what happened to stock prices when those debtors couldn't pay their bills. Taken together, this all suggests that the vast majority of riskier loans approved in recent years may literally be built on a "house of cards".

Banks are not immune from a shakeout in the real estate market either. Many would say the banking system is more levered to the housing market than ever before (perhaps as much as 50% more than it was in 1990 when the US real estate market experienced its last period of turmoil). Sure there are claims that these banks have diversified away their risks to foreign entities and hedge funds, but in these times of shenanigans and less than opaque accounting practices, would anyone really want to trust them? If these numbers are real, and given that the S&P500 companies overall derived about one-quarter of their earnings from finance-related activities in 2005, I would be very concerned that a problem in the housing industry could set off a major slide in the stock indexes as well.

Income Ratios

Median US home prices in mid-2005 were around five times median household incomes. Thirty years earlier this ratio was about 3.3, according to the National Association of Homebuilders. What's alarming is that many more women are in the workforce now than there were 30 years ago (and earning more money), so to really compare apples-to-apples, these numbers must be normalized by removing a portion of household income. This normalization has the effect of driving the ratio much higher today than it already is. The ratio today is the best of all worlds in that it occurs during a period in which the percentage of women in the work-force is near a peak (i.e. a maximized level of dual-income households), interest rates were at their lowest in 40 years, and the most favorable tax policy for home ownership in decades was in effect. Things can only get worse from here, and just as this ratio was driven higher on the way up, it could be magnified on the way down by the opposing forces. Although unlikely, the ratio could ultimately return to its prior lows.

Affordability

Various housing affordability trackers began revealing major cracks in the housing market in 2004, when affordability fell to its lowest levels since the 1989 to 1991 period. By late 2005, several high-flying real estate markets in California had become so unaffordable that an average family could afford to own less than one-half of a house. Homes in several states had become so unaffordable that over half of new mortgages granted in those states were of the adjustable-rate variety. My affordability data analysis in early 2006 suggested that the median home in the New York metropolitan area was as much as 50% overvalued. At that time, just about the only good thing I could say about the New York real estate market for prospective buyers was that the most unaffordable markets tended to be in California.

Some indicators show that the US real estate market is still at a median level of affordability, and many real estate industry professionals use such data to suggest that the market is not in a bubble. One must remember, however, that there are pockets throughout the US which have not participated in the astronomical appreciation, and are therefore helping to give the appearance that affordability may still be reasonable. This unfortunately will not help the markets which have experienced hyper-growth, as they will nevertheless go through either painful corrections or medium- to long-term stalls as affordability continues to fall dramatically with the increase in interest rates.

Real Inflation Revisited

Until 1983, the Bureau of Labor Statistics (the agency that calculates the Consumer Price Index or CPI) measured housing inflation by monitoring the cost of owning a home. The Bureau then decided that a more accurate reflection of the cost of housing was how much it cost to rent, rather than to own. The reason for this change was that while over an extended period of time the two tended to move together, the cost of owning was subject to wild short-term cycles, whereas changes in renting costs resulted in much smoother numbers. This change turned out to be a big reason for the recent low inflation numbers, as the cost of owning has greatly outpaced the cost of renting since the late 1990's. The last decade has seen average annual rent increases of about 3% versus average annual housing ownership cost increases of about 7%. One of three things must therefore happen at this point. The cost of ownership has to decrease a lot, or the cost of renting needs to increase greatly, or they must both move toward each other. The reason there must be a significant change in this relationship is because nearly 70% of households now own their homes, and as such, home ownership now has a much more dramatic effect on "real" inflation than it did in the past. Housing makes up around one-quarter of the CPI, its largest component. This means that unless the cost of renting meets up with the cost of owning, the Bureau may eventually be forced to change its method for calculating the housing component of the CPI to reflect the change in the relationship between the two.

As stated earlier, the Bureau switched from ownership costs to renting costs in 1983, but may now be forced to switch back or at least to arrive at a blend of the two in order to more accurately reflect what is truly happening with the cost of shelter in the US. The only other option is for the Fed and other government bodies to take action to bring down the cost of ownership so that the cost of ownership is somewhat more closely aligned with the cost of renting. This is why I believe the Fed will keep raising interest rates to pop the real estate bubble, even if the numbers show that inflation is tamed. The published inflation numbers are based on an outdated methodology, which does not truly reflect the real inflation numbers today. Earlier in the book, I discussed today's environment of "stealth" inflation.

Now is time to evaluate the real contribution of the cost of housing to the CPI. Let's do a quick calculation and adjust the inflation cost of renting (3%) and the inflation cost of owning (7%) using an appropriately weighted formula:

$$(70\% \times 7\%) + (30\% \times 3\%) = {\sim}6\%$$

In this equation, 70% represents the percent of households which own their homes, and 30% represents those renting. This more accurate representation of housing inflation would then make up one-quarter of CPI, and have the net effect of adding close to a full percentage point to the stated CPI of each of the years of the last decade, on average. This higher and truer inflation number is very possibly the number Greenspan was using and Bernanke is using behind the scenes to determine when the Fed gets to neutral on interest rates. Let's not forget that the other components which make up inflation tend to be understated as well, and therefore the real inflation rate is even higher. This suggests to me that if the Fed is truly intent on doing its job, it will continue raising interest rates to a level which is higher than what most people expect. These higher rates should ultimately help to cool things down, and eventually bring the cost of owning back into equilibrium with the cost of renting.

Television

It was mid-2005, and the topic of that day's normally notoriously bullish show was the real estate bubble. To my surprise, the panelists who were normally bullish were sounding pretty bearish. The lone "bull" on the show mentioned that she was selling her home. What none of the other panelists asked her was why she was selling if she was bullish. Wouldn't someone who thinks the market is going up, hold onto her home, or at least trade it in for another home? Apparently, this panelist was planning on selling, and didn't appear to have further reinvestment plans for her newfound wealth. When I think about that show, I am still amazed that she would express two such contradictory views, and I am even more amazed that none of the other panelists or the host even called her on the blatant contradiction. It is very sad that this is the quality of experts the media is putting in front of viewers, and equally sad that this is how many of the hosts of such shows operate. Once again, the lesson is that many of these people on television are entertainers, and are not to be trusted for advice.

For all the people who give bad advice, let's be thankful for the few who actually try to help. Fast forward to *The Suzie Orman Show* in late October, 2005, as she interviewed people concerning the real estate market. One woman stated that she wanted to get into the real estate market before the crash. Suzie, who is a very bright woman, explained to this woman that what she said made no sense. Suzie explained that if this woman believed that the market was about to crash, she should not want to get into it, but should be running away from it. Sadly, the woman who made that statement did not appear to understand what Suzie was telling her, and this woman is representative of many of the buyers who have been driving the market over the last couple of years. Unfortunately for them, in many cases they are the same people who got into the stock market right before it crashed in 2000.

One investor who successfully navigated the stock market crash of 1929 was widely quoted as having told his associates that he knew it was time to get out of the market when his shoe shiner started giving him stock tips. This is a lesson which every investor should never forget.

Traders and Brokers

One large group cashing in on the real estate bubble is the investors who live in their residences and move every few years. If married and filing jointly, they pay no taxes on the first $500 thousand of their gain (if single, the exemption is on the first $250 thousand). These people do take a risk each time they trade into a new home, as prices could fall. But, at least they took their tax free gains once, twice, or maybe three times if they've been doing this every few years.

But the real winners are the real estate brokers. This is because those savvy homeowners who trade in their homes every few years generally enlist the services of a real estate broker. So even if only 5% of the home owning population pulls this maneuver every few years, the total number of transactions soars. Even with an increasing number of brokers entering the field as the market rises, those who are already established receive the lion's share of the business, and their compensation soars along with the higher commissions which rise with the rising value of the underlying real estate.

Estimates suggest that total commission revenue on residential real estate in the US increased by 50% between 2000 and 2004 to roughly $60 billion. This is a large chunk of change and the people in this industry do not want to see it go away. Real estate brokers (like many stock brokers and financial advisors) earn a commission based on the value of what they sell, so the higher the prices of the products they sell, the more they get paid. And they get paid even if they cause the home buyer to lose money! Of note is that until ten years ago, when real estate started vastly outpacing inflation, real estate agents' compensation was essentially indexed to inflation, as it was tied to a 6% commission. Since real estate appreciation has outpaced stated inflation by a three-to-one margin in recent years, agents' compensation has soared on a relative basis. Using this inflation-adjusted basis, agents are making far more now than in recent history, and maybe ever.

Appraisers

One current trend in the real estate market is that many appraisers have been increasing their assessments of valuations on properties for sale. Pressure (direct and/or indirect) to engage in this practice could come from mortgage brokers, loan officers and/or real estate agents. Higher assessed value means higher commissions for all of them, so they all have an interest in pushing values up. If this is occurring, does it sound familiar? Think 1999/2000 stock market.

During the 1999/2000 period, stock analysts were under enormous pressure to give all individual stocks the nod. Figures showed that for a period of time, 99% of ratings were "buy" or "hold" with less than 1% being "sell". Much of the pressure may have come from Wall Street management which wanted stocks to go up. Upwardly mobile stocks help to generate more underwriting business from clients, and the Wall Street firms themselves may have been pressured by executives of those same banking client companies who wanted to see their stock prices go up. Wall Street analysts may also have been hoping for high level positions, and therefore may have doled out favors in hopes of eventual invitations to join the executive suites of their client companies. What's changed is that instead of the stock market, it may now be the real estate market, and instead of it being the Wall Street firms and their client companies, it may now be the mortgage brokers, loan officers, and real estate agents. The real estate industry is huge, and many people have an interest in seeing the market rise. And we all remember how things ended following 1999/2000, when everybody wanted the stock market to keep rising.

House Owners, Not Home Owners

You're probably already asking yourself what the difference is between a house owner and a homeowner, and it's a very good question. I define "house owners" as those who own assets. A house owner doesn't refer to a house as a home because he/she doesn't live there and doesn't feel that it is a home. A house owner looks at a house as an investment property, which is not much different than how he/she looks at a stock or a bond. To the house owner, a house is something to be bought and sold (and/or rented, and perhaps occasionally used), perhaps even traded on an annual or monthly basis.

"Homeowners" refers to the class of owners who make their properties their homes. Under normal circumstances, a homeowner's intention is to remain in a home alone or with family and/or friends for at least a few years. House owners are almost always homeowners as well, with the difference being that generally only one or two (or possibly three) of their houses are actually also their homes. The rest of their houses are investments. Alas, when the number of houses owned climbs to a certain percentage of the total of homes and houses owned, the real estate market has gotten into dangerous territory. This can be expressed as a simple formula which I call the "house ownership ratio":

(houses owned)/(houses owned + homes owned) = house ownership ratio

Consider that in late 2005, many markets in California and Florida (with a smattering of other states' local markets) showed the house ownership ratio in the 20% range, and the market has likely reached the danger zone. Nobody knows what these house owners (investors and speculators) will do now that the real estate markets are showing signs of softening, but if past is prologue, then the most savvy investors will sell, leaving the rest of population to ponder and debate while riding asset prices down to some more realistic valuation level.

Housing Starts

Housing starts figures have evolved from boom-bust cycles to steady growth, or at least that's what many in the real estate industry would like the homeowner to believe. Just because the market hasn't seen any major volatility in 15 years doesn't mean volatility has disappeared. In fact, to the contrary, the real estate market behaves like any other investment market, and in particular, one needs to look no further than the stock market for guidance. Stock market volatility subsides and calm sweeps the markets just before those markets experience a massive spike in volatility, often accompanied by a large correction. It turns out that the housing market is no stranger to volatility. The US housing market experienced average drops of about 50% in housing starts during the busts of 1972-1975, 1978-1982 and 1987-1991.

In the past decade there have been tremendous changes in the home-construction industry, and these changes will have a major effect on housing starts in the future. In past times, when the industry was dominated by smaller mom-and-pop builders, and their small fortunes were on the line, builders were far more cautious. At the first signs of overbuilding or rising interest rates, those builders would slow things down, because if they kept building and conditions rapidly deteriorated, they could be at risk of losing everything. Remember, their personal fortunes were on the line. Today's home-construction industry looks nothing like that. Today, there are several large, very well capitalized public companies which control half the market. The executives who run these companies want to grow as rapidly as they can so that their company stock prices go up, and they can sell shares at great profit (their entire personal fortunes are rarely on the line).

In the event demand for new homes falls, the home building game then becomes market share. The large companies will simply attract new buyers by dropping their selling prices. As they lower prices, they can potentially gain market share, and even though the cost per home and profit per home may be lower, they will still have the potential to make more revenue and profit overall. An analogous situation would be that of Wal-Mart, which lowered its prices, but kept growing in the 1970's, 80's, and 90's by taking market share from everyone else.

So why are investors focused on housing starts to measure the health of the real estate market? In the current atmosphere, this is an outdated methodology with which to gage the health of the housing market. Housing starts can remain stable and even increase, while average- and median-home values decline. So it appears to me that the new home starts statistic is only useful as one method of assessing the health of the home building industry itself.

Building industry profits per home built is one of the most relevant gages of the health of the real estate market, and when that profit begins to fall, it may be a long way to the bottom. When profits per home falls, this means that builders must give their clients more for less, which means that existing homeowners who are attempting to sell may not be able to offer the same value. They could therefore be forced to drop their prices, ushering in the real estate market decline. The essential point I am making is that the market has entered a phase in which there is a decoupling of housing starts figures and the value of real estate. How it all plays out remains to be seen and is dependent on many variables, but the model has changed forever.

This all reminds me of a trip I took to Turkey in 2000. As I traveled around the country, I repeatedly saw buildings of all shapes and sizes in an unfinished state. I grew more and more perplexed as I realized that there could have been millions of unfinished housing units. I began asking questions and was given a litany of reasons which really did not justify what I was seeing, until I was told that the government offered some sort of subsidy to builders which only remained in effect as long as a building was unfinished. So to take advantage of these subsidies, the builders left a great number of buildings unfinished. The real estate market and the stock market were booming. But I came back from my trip wondering what month the day of reckoning would come for Turkey. Not to my surprise, the day of reckoning was just a few months away, at which time its markets collapsed.

Who's Buying?

Nationwide, the US has a household ownership rate of almost 70% and a rental housing market which has plenty of availability. These figures, along with population growth simply do not support anything beyond minimal growth in the housing stock of the country. So who is buying all these new homes?

Realtors Association figures showed that in 2004 over 8% of all home purchases were as investments and about 5% as vacation homes. Assuming half of these owners of investment properties are seasoned investors and they immediately cash out at the first sign of a drop in prices, they will create a very significant market drop which will set off a larger-scale decline.

While in many cases second homes can provide stability, the reverse can also be true. Many second-home owners make a quick killing on their first home, and only months or years later, roll their gains into a second home in hopes of riding the real estate boom to instant prosperity. But if conditions rapidly deteriorate, they could be forced to rid themselves of those homes. This, of course, would contribute to a decline in home values across the country. Further, the real estate industry's perpetuators of myths love to tell people that the market is regional, and that one way of diversifying is to buy homes in different geographic areas. Unfortunately, however, when everyone follows this advice, the market is no longer regional.

Another group that has raised some attention lately is seniors. Senior heads of households with mortgage debt had been increasing at an alarming rate through

2005. While people living longer and starting families later could account for some of this, a greater reason for this growth rate is likely an attempt on the part of these homeowners to ride the housing boom to security. Unfortunately, as this number increases, so too does the risk that with a real estate bust, they will be more dependent on the government and on their offspring to make ends meet. Like most other homeowners, it is likely they have been using increasing home equity to fund much of their consumption, and have not planned for a sharp fall-off in the value of their homes.

It is estimated that the number of illegal immigrants in the US more than doubled to 12 million from 1995 to 2005. By the end of 2005, estimates suggested that "illegals" held as many as 5% of all jobs in the US. To illustrate how dependent the US economy had become on them, prosecutions of employers of "illegals" fell to close to nil in 2005! "Illegals" need places to live, and with the rapid increase in "not fully documented lending", it should be of no surprise that they have been buying homes, which with creative financing can end up being more affordable on a monthly basis than renting. Nobody knows how many illegal immigrants are homeowners, but they certainly have contributed to the run-up in prices.

Let's examine the scenario of a popping real estate bubble. When the bubble pops and the economy takes a hit, as the value of illegals' homes falls to levels below the amounts they owe on the homes, many of them will simply disappear. Recall that many loans are not fully documented. Many of these illegals will go back to their native countries if things get really tough in the US. Many will relocate to other parts of the US for better opportunities, and just walk away from their homes and debts. After all, if their mortgages are not fully documented to begin with and many of these people have false identification, they will never be tracked down. They will likely assume new identities and start all over again, as their homes are added to the bloated home inventory numbers. Unfortunately for US citizens who were lured into the real estate market, the outcome will not be so good. With tougher bankruptcy laws passed, they will be liable for their mortgages and may have negative net worth for years to come.

Where Are the Bubbles?

With increasing talk concerning the location of real estate bubbles, all sorts of gages are being developed by lenders, government agencies, bankers, brokers, and others to better navigate these minefields. This concern has resulted in various tabulations ranking the riskiest markets in the US. One interesting outcome from all of this is that the most inflated local markets often differ from list to list. Many people would say that because there is little agreement on where the bubbles are, by definition this means the bubbles do not exist. I see things the other way. I would prefer that all the lists agree. This would tell me that there are bubbles in only a few cities, and that the rest of the market may be spared a correction. Unfortunately, the lack of agreement suggests to me that there are bubbles scattered all over the country, and this could very well lead to what may be the first time in recent US history that the median price of real estate actually falls year-over-year. If this were to occur, it would set a very dangerous precedent and severely puncture the bloated confidence of the US homeowner.

There are differing methodologies used in attempts to determine whether markets are overvalued and by how much they are overvalued. A ratio of the share of US housing value in a particular market to share of total US population can give an indication of relative valuation of that market, because any real estate market requires people in that market to occupy its homes. Ratios for three major markets (based on FDIC numbers from mid-2005) come to approximately 1.3, 2.1, and 3.1 for Chicago, New York, and San Francisco, respectively. When the market finally turns, all the major coastal markets will be vulnerable, and could potentially see their ratios fall to levels in a range of 1.25 to 1.5, which would still allow for a more realistic premium over the national average. This suggests that New York could come down by about one-third, and San Francisco could possibly fall by over 50%, relative to the national average. But Chicago is also likely to undergo a serious correction, as it is not a coastal city, and therefore has a lot of room for building. I should stress, however, that these are just approximations, and the numbers therefore suggest only possible outcomes.

Manhattan Real Estate

Manhattan home prices are a good indicator as to how overvalued real estate prices are in many local markets. This is because in many studies of the most overvalued markets in the country, Manhattan is not at the top of the list, but is perhaps in the second tier of overpriced markets.

Actual prices are one means of comparison, but are not as meaningful as inflation-adjusted prices when comparing real estate values from one period to another. From the last real estate top to the current peak in 2005, Manhattan's average inflation-adjusted price per square foot was reportedly up approximately 35 to 40%. Of course Manhattan has become much safer and cleaner, and therefore presumably more desirable a place to live, but the number of housing units has also increased rapidly to accommodate the increased demand. Given that all variables move in reaction to all other variables and the market behaves efficiently, the inflation-adjusted unit cost should revert to a mean number over a period of time.

Let's explore what happens when the market ultimately reverses course. Prices fell over 40% in real terms from peak to trough during the last correction, which ran its course by the mid-1990's. Nothing is preventing the market from dropping a similar magnitude from today's highs, and such a drop would take the market back to approximately the 1999 level. But since the market is 35 to 40% more expensive today in real terms than it was at the peak of the last cycle, it could potentially fall far more than 40% this time (coincidentally this 40% figure is approximately the same magnitude of correction experienced by Los Angeles in the early-1990's). And let's remember that Manhattan is not even considered one of the grossly overvalued markets.

1988

It was 1988 and I had once again begun my search for a condo in the Boston area. I was working as an engineer for General Electric, and attending night school in the Boston University MBA program, so I generally limited my search to the summers, when I had more time. I had been out looking during the summer of 1987 and even a little in 1986 before that. By now prices had risen to the point that I began to panic, wondering how I could ever afford a nice 2-bedroom condo on an engineer's salary. Even as I expanded my search to one-bedrooms, I just felt that something was incredibly wrong when an engineer at a top firm couldn't afford a 2-bedroom condo. Fortunately, I didn't have to worry much longer. It wouldn't be long before the real estate correction was in full force. I did not buy a condo, and in 1990, I returned to New York as I witnessed real estate prices falling throughout the northeast and much of the rest of the country.

The real estate industry had driven prices up to unsustainable levels for all the same reasons that a stock market bubble forms. Accompanying the bubble were all the familiar arguments. So the next time someone tells you that "this time it's different", remind them that "the more things change, the more they stay the same".

"Real" Real Estate

Some recent real estate buyers have been fortunate, and have posted triple-digit returns on the values of their homes in just a few short years, and many more times on the value of their initial investments (provided they have cashed in their gains). But one must always remember that there will be periods when the market falls, because real estate markets are cyclical. There were multi-year periods in the early 1980's and again in the early 1990's in which the overall US real estate market experienced real losses in the double-digits, in percentage terms. For a 50-year period from 1894 to 1944, people who owned homes in the US did not fare very well at all. In real terms, their homes lost one-third of their values, according to a study from Case-Shiller. This, more than anything else, should put to bed the myth that US median home values never go down.

In *Irrational Exuberance*, Robert Shiller created a graph showing inflation-adjusted US housing prices going back to 1890. The real estate market briefly touched 125% (where 100% is inflation trendline) in the mid 1890's, and again in the late 1970's and late 1980's. The market busted through that 125% milestone in the late 1990's, and was over 180% by 2005! Until the most recent decade, the great struggle was for housing prices to just keep slightly ahead of inflation.

The end result of the current bubble will most likely be a substantial drop in real estate values, and a reversion back to the mean of gains which slightly exceed inflation. Of course, however, there could be an exception. As I have discussed, the true inflation rate in recent years may not have been 1 to 3% as is generally stated, but in fact something much higher (what I referred to earlier as stealth or real inflation, in the range of 5% to 7%). And maybe the consumer was a lot smarter than Greenspan gave him credit for being. Perhaps the consumer knew the true inflation rate was higher than the stated rate, and reacted by bidding up the price of homes as a hedge against this inflation.

Unfortunately (or fortunately, depending on your viewpoint), it really doesn't matter what rationale was used to bid the prices of real estate up in the first place, because as interest rates rise, and credit standards tighten, we will likely witness a large-scale correction. There is a possibility that a reversion to the mean could cause a correction of as much as 60% in some markets, adjusted for inflation. This would not be completely unexpected by those who recall recent stock market history when the Nasdaq lost 80% and even the Dow lost 40% in just a two-to-three year period. In real terms, the losses were even worse, as the money tied up in those assets could have been earning risk-free interest elsewhere. It is essential to realize that things can happen very quickly going up, and they can happen just as quickly going down.

Should the feared collapse in the real estate market come, the result could be a downward spiral in prices, which could possibly trigger a vicious cycle of decreasing stock market and real estate prices, similar to what Japan experienced in the 1990's and early 2000's. I am not implying that this is how events will play out. I do believe, however, that people who have everything riding on real estate are likely to get burned. Everybody should have a substantial percent of their assets in safe cash investments (money-market funds, short-term government securities, etc.).

More Studies

There are always studies being done on the real estate market just as there are for all the investment markets. It is up to the investor then to try to read between the lines to project best case and worst case scenarios to determine real risk.

Under normal circumstances, real estate declines can take place in various regions of the US for an assortment of reasons. But we are not in normal times. It is unclear how the national market would respond to a major rise in interest rates following a massive run-up in prices brought on by several years of record low rates and super-relaxed lending standards. Studies for recent decades have tended to focus on local market declines which occurred as the total US market was in a long-term bull market, and therefore those markets may have been pulled back up by the rest of the US market (recall the old saying once again that a rising tide lifts all ships). Should the total US market go into bear mode, data from the past few decades could be worthless, and the more vulnerable local markets could be especially hard hit.

Mortgage Debt

One of the most startling relationships I've observed concerns that of real estate values and mortgage debt. Estimates show that from 2000 to 2005, total mortgage debt in the US rose close to the same percentage as did the total value of real estate. This reminds me of 1929, when buying stocks on margin was so prevalent that much of the gain in the market was funded by risky loans to investors who had thrown caution to the wind.

Everything is wonderful for market participants as long as the market is rising, but those market participants need to think about what might happen when the market falls. The executives at public corporations in the housing industry will have likely cashed out plenty in the form of huge compensation packages, so they should be just fine. Successful real estate agents, appraisers, and others in the industry will have already been paid for their work during the boom years. The small investor and the homeowner, however, will have personally signed for large amounts of debt. And a common escape maneuver used by the little guy in the last downturn (bankruptcy) will not offer the same advantages this time around due to the more stringent bankruptcy laws.

The New Margin

I watched a television talk show in mid-2005, and one guest was talking about how easy it was to make money in real estate. Prices are going up 20% a year, he said, so what you do is take $5 thousand, put it down on a highly leveraged mortgage, and as simple as that you can make 100% to 400% a year on your money. But he never addressed what could happen if things turn around, and prices fall.

Should prices fall considerably and stay down for a while, forcing people to start selling, a downward spiral could result. The banks and other lenders, who so willingly lent money to high-risk clients, would expect full payment on the money owed to them. When borrowers who did not save money (because they relied on their homes for savings) cannot keep up with their mortgage payments, the lenders will foreclose on their homes. To me, this is starting to sound more and more like the stock market of 1929, which was propelled higher and higher through "margin" buying before ultimately falling like the house of cards it was. The lose margin requirements for purchasing stocks at that time is shockingly similar to the availability of easy money for real estate today. By certain measures, it's even worse today. It is now generally accepted knowledge that greater than 50% of new mortgages in California are of the interest only variety, and many are low doc, no doc's and NINA's.

Deteriorating Lending Standards

Even as Greenspan raised interest rates in an attempt to cool the housing market, the net percentage of banks tightening mortgage lending standards remained fairly stagnant through 2005, based on data from the Federal Reserve. And who knows what's going on with the other lenders.

Let's analyze why there had been no real change in lending standards through 2005. Executives don't want to lose business to competitors, so when a competitor loosens its lending standards, the executives of another lender decide to loosen theirs as well. They understand that to a large degree their own wealth is closely tied to the growth and profitability of the company they run. They also recognize that the current real estate cycle will last for only so long, and that when it comes to an end, they could forgo bonuses, raises, and maybe even their jobs. They understand that their mortgages are repackaged into new financial instruments and sold to the greater universe of bond investors, which essentially makes all investors and the US government their partners. So their downside risk in relaxing lending standards is essentially hedged away to everybody else, whereas their upside belongs fully to themselves and to the shareholders in their company.

Any unbiased observer would have to conclude that these executives would be foolish to tighten standards while their competitors loosened. A few good companies in similar predicaments in varying industries have done the right thing in similar situations, and have usually paid the price in the form of lost market share, which in some cases started downward spirals in business from which those companies never recovered. So unless a government agency steps up to the plate and regulates this industry, the standards will not be tightened. To further illustrate this argument, one needs only to recall the reckless behavior of the executives of various types of public companies during the recent stock market bubble and in its aftermath.

Interest Rates

The Fed has been continuously raising interest rates for close to two years, as it attempts to send a message to the investment markets. One year Treasury's, one-year adjustables, money market rates, bank interest rates, and all others are responding, as they move up along a linear trend line. These trends have all been in place since at least early 2004, and as long as none are broken to the downside, it is a near certainty interest rates will continue rising, and the end result will be a leveling off or drop in real estate values. Those values will continue dropping until some point in time after these interest rate trendlines are broken to the downside.

Secure?

It was mid-2005 that I heard the most insane argument yet of why real estate prices were secure. A man on television stated that about 33% of US homeowners own their homes outright, and another 50% or so have fixed-rate mortgages, so a very small percentage are in the newer exotic mortgages. That was the basis for this pundit's argument that an increase in interest rates would have little effect on the prices of real estate. I would love to have been able to question that guest on this premier business show, and I don't understand why the hosts of these shows don't ask tougher questions. The first thing I would have asked that guest was to explain to me why the stock market fell by so much from its highs of 2000, when a far greater percentage of stocks were owned outright and very little was bought on margin. Everybody should be thinking about the great myth which he was attempting to perpetuate.

An acceptable argument which this "expert" might have made would be that the average value of real estate would not go to zero, or rather that there would be a "floor" below which that average value would never go. That floor might be 80%, 70%, 50%, or some other fraction of its current levels.

Cooling

Reports have been hitting the press since late 2005, showing applications for home purchase loans had fallen by double-digit percentage points from earlier in the year, and that the average price of new and existing homes had fallen in the final quarter of 2005. Now that fewer people are in the market for homes, and the builders and savvy sellers started lowering prices, panicky sellers will follow. Prices could drop precipitously in the race to divest.

Should the trend continue, it would be a major psychological blow to the typical homeowner, as for the first time in many years, that homeowner will feel as though he/she had become less wealthy. This reverse wealth effect could have dire consequences for the economy, depending on how a range of activities play out going forward.

How Far Might It Fall?

A number of countries from various parts of the world have seen far more significant gains in their real estate markets than has the US. An optimist will look at such data and say the US real estate market is not overvalued, and that it has much more to go to catch up with the rest of the world. The realist will say, ah, but remember how the Nasdaq doubled in one year, and recall how the optimists said how much further the Dow would go in light of the Nasdaq gains. Subsequently, the Nasdaq fell 80% and the Dow fell about 40%. So maybe South

Africa will fall 60% and the US 40%, in real terms. For someone who recently bought into this market, 40% is a long way down.

Wealthy Americans Cut Back

The World Wealth Report from Cap Gemini and Merrill Lynch & Co showed that Americans with greater than $1 million in liquid assets cut their real estate holdings from 17% of total assets in 2003 to 13% in 2004, on the heels of an increase from 2002 to 2003. I would guess that the percentage has fallen further in 2005.

What do the rich know that the rest of the population doesn't?

Remember the man in the TV commercials over the years who answers; "how do you think I got so rich?" in response to someone who asks him why he spends so little money on a particular product when he is so rich. The rich have always been accused of being lots of things, but being stupid has never been one of them. So if they have been reducing their allocation of wealth to real estate since 2003, then the real estate market is currently truly on the last legs of its expansion. Other surveys and analyses of the "smart" money have yielded similar results. Such surveys had shown in mid-2005 that the smart money felt the top of the real estate market had already been reached. And anyone who ignores the opinion of the smart money is a fool.

I know of people who have 50%, 80%, 100%, and even more than 100% (net debtors) of their wealth in real estate. So why did the rich only have 13% of their wealth in it in 2004? A very meaningful number might be the percent allocation of personal wealth which people in the real estate business have tied up in real estate. If such a study were ever commissioned, I would wager that this number would be far lower than that of the average homeowner, which brings me back to the stock market of early 2000. I knew people who had close to 100% of their wealth in the stock market in early 2000, and they took severe blows when the market crashed. Even while all the investment firms were recommending clients hold 50 to 75% of their money in stocks, individuals at those firms on average were far more insulated against the stock market. In many ways real estate has become the new stock market. In fact, I believe it has become the new 1929 stock market, although not as overvalued as that stock market was.

If you want to get rich, think like the rich. The rich had 13% of their wealth in real estate in 2004. The market is a lot closer to the top of this cycle than it is to the bottom.

Cycles

Just as I earlier wrote about stock market cycles, there is also a real estate cycle to be aware of. The real estate cycle is not quite as developed as the various and intricate stock market cycles for lots of reasons, but it is important to understand that it exists. It too has been written and talked about extensively, and is considered common knowledge by those in the know. There is approximately an eighteen- to twenty-year cycle of local lows and local highs with a few smaller gyrations in between, and according to my calculations, the last local top was to occur around 2004 to 2006. You are probably reading this book in 2006 or later, so chances are that we are on our way down from the top in 2005.

International Housing Boom?

Historical numbers generally can give a good indication of what is likely to occur in the future. Historically, the US market has risen approximately 1-2 percentage points per year above inflation. Some other nations' markets have appreciated at a much greater rate and a few others have lagged. Just as there are local bubbles in the US, there are local bubbles throughout the world. These bubbles can be regional (i.e. Asian) or country-specific. We can break these bubbles down further by identifying them as either country-specific within a region (i.e. China) or locale-specific within a country (Shanghai). The point is that there are several types of real estate bubbles which have popped or are about to pop. They are regions within countries, countries within regions, and regions of the world, and they are all happening together. Almost everyone who can afford to buy real estate is already in this game. And when the game ends, buyers from other regions and countries may not have the availability of funds or the appetite for risk to come into new regions and countries to buy real estate. Without outsiders to come to the rescue of declining markets, the contagion will spread throughout the world as panic buying turns into panic selling. It is possible however that long-term underperforming markets could see price stabilization as value buyers roll their gains over to such markets.

When the greater correction scenario unfolds, there is likely to be one of two consequences. The first is that the unwinding of the real estate bubble will result in less consumer purchasing power, which will result in lower economic activity (likely resulting in recession), and as consumers and investors seek out the safety of government-backed Treasuries now paying ever-higher interest rates, the real estate and stock markets will undergo short- to medium-term declines. The second scenario is that investors and consumers who cash out in time decide to roll their wealth into stock markets. These stock markets could then rise, helping to cushion the real estate debacle, as the new wealth effect created by this rollover into stocks could give people a new vehicle from which to draw spending funds. Such a scenario would have to be self-perpetuating, however, as the spending would drive stocks higher, creating a continued wealth effect, which would then drive spending, and so on. I believe this scenario is unlikely to continue, however, unless the Fed-equivalents of countries throughout the world began lowering interest rates once again. One thing to keep in mind, however, is that the stock markets are still in an echo bubble, and therefore, may still have years left to unwind, themselves. The possibility exists that the world or significant parts of the world could be heading into a period of stagnation, not that dissimilar to what Japan experienced since the popping of its dual bubbles in 1990.

There is also another way of interpreting international data showing massive run-ups in other countries' real estate markets. For quite some time, there were few very desirable countries in which to own real estate. The US was one of these places, and given the means, many people from other countries would gladly have bought in the US, theoretically helping to push up real estate prices. Now, there are lots of up-and-coming places to own. Many of the same people who only ten years ago would have preferred to buy in the US would now choose to do so elsewhere. A rational person should be thinking that if all those other places have become much more desirable, and fewer people desire to be in the US, then who will be left to buy in the US market. The answer is that to some extent this should be a zero-sum game, in which the most desirable places to live attract the people with the most money to spend, and those markets get bid up. But that is not what is happening. What is happening is that since the Fed opened the money spigots, money has flowed throughout the world, and that money has combined with deteriorated lending standards to create a world-wide real estate bubble, the likes of which the world has never seen before.

2006

Figures for the January real estate market are out and they are not very encouraging. Figures showed that inventory had grown by about 100% in many US bubble markets. Some reports showed inventories to be at ten-year highs. The fact that January was one of the warmest on record with the lowest levels of snowfall is not a good omen either. Normally such an increase in inventories might be blamed on the weather, but this time the good weather should have actually generated a decrease in inventory. Even worse, it was announced that new units started actually rose. Somebody who doesn't do the math might think this is good, but anyone who takes the time to think for just a moment will see that all this does is adds more inventory to the already high levels, which is not good for price stability. These are major signs of things to come.

5

ENERGY

Energy Bubble?

Let's face the facts. Whether the US produces goods or China produces goods, everyone still needs energy to make those goods and to transport those goods (not to mention energy used in the services sectors, which is far higher than most people believe and accounts for an ever-increasing percent of energy usage).

Over the past few years, the prices for energy derived from depletable resources have gone into hyper-growth mode. Natural gas in particular moved so rapidly to the upside, that it went far beyond the typical hyperbolic-bubble pattern which one would normally see. Having gone from about $5 to $15 per million BTU's in just a year, it already came crashing back to earth. The US got very lucky in late 2005 with one of the warmest winters on record, but if oil prices remain high and winters grow colder in the next few years, the price of natural gas will once again rise.

Gasoline and heating oil prices have been following classic bubble patterns. It is very possible that peaks were reached in late 2005, but we won't know for sure until a few critical factors play themselves out. The price of oil needs to come down to the $40 range for me to be fairly certain the highs of 2005 won't be breached in the next few years. A lot of this depends on what the Fed does with interest rates to control the world's appetite for this commodity. It was recently reported that China's oil imports in January, 2006 rose by 70% year-over-year. Clearly this does not bode well for the price of oil in the near term, and if this type of growth continues, the price of oil could continue along its recent hyperbolic path and move above $100 by 2007. Again, it all depends on how tough the Fed is willing to get.

US Energy Consumption

In order to understand the energy situation in the US, one needs to know what the usage figures are today. To put things in perspective, the US Energy Information Administration released figures for 2005 which show the big three energy sources for the US to be oil, coal and natural gas, coming in at approximately 40%, 23%, and 23%, respectively. The balance of energy is derived from other sources, just over half of which is nuclear. Since oil is the largest source and its price has not come down, let's focus on the forces playing out in the oil market.

The US accounts for 4% of the world's population, but burns 25% of the world's oil, based on figures from the Energy Information Administration. This may go far in explaining why we prefer to exhaust the rest of the world's oil supply before our own. It should be noted that although the US is one of the worst offenders (perhaps the worst) many developed nations are close behind.

The Energy Information Administration has shown that oil imports as a percentage of total oil consumption in the US has increased from about 45% in 1990 to near 65% by mid-2005. In other words, US foreign oil dependency has increased by about 44% in these 15 short years. At the current rate, by 2020, we could be importing about 90% of our oil. This is not a good thing, because it forecasts a potential future of great inflation and possibly many large-scale international wars over oil. The disruptions caused by either of these events would bring the world's stock markets to their knees.

The Economics and Politics of Oil

Consider the following pertaining to the oil industry. The cost of oil has fallen dramatically during brief periods throughout history thanks to great improvements in oil extraction technologies and efficiency, along with the benefits of economies of scale. Taken together, this has allowed the price of oil to remain in a trading range in real dollar terms, albeit with fluctuations along the way. This suggests that assuming technology and efficiency continue to improve, oil is probably near a fair price level, and that if events play out the way they have historically, its price will fall considerably before rising again. But, of course, this only holds for as long as there is oil in the ground. Naturally, when we truly begin nearing the depletion of oil reserves, the price will skyrocket unless there are viable, alternative energy sources available.

Recent history has shown that estimated and proven oil reserves continue to rise at greater rates than many experts believed. Some estimates of oil in the US alone are equal to the amount of oil in all of OPEC combined. Nobody can know with any real certainty, because every national government has interests in both under-reporting and over-reporting their reserves for various political and economic reasons, and whenever a government needs to, it can shift from one stance to the other. When I evaluate all the data available to me (and you), I conclude that the world will not run out of oil anytime in the near future (meaning at least 50 years, even at current growth rates). Further, as supply constricts and prices rise, it will become more financially feasible to extract oil (and/or other resources) from challenging sources, like shale rocks, tar sands, arctic climates, deep water, volcanic areas, and others. At some point in time, there may even be an oil glut, causing the price of oil to fall precipitously, if history is any guide. Technological advances will allow for advanced oil recovery, but also will permit the development of alternative energy sources, simultaneously. For myriad reasons (national security, environmentalist concerns, etc.), the US government seems to prefer to exhaust supplies from other nations prior to exhausting its own. But what this suggests is that as long as oil demand grows in a slow and controlled fashion, all these problems should take care of themselves (at least for a balanced economy like the US).

When demand growth steadily exceeds supply growth is when problems develop. This is why the Fed must get involved at the first signs of supply-demand imbalances, and quickly act to slow demand, or else be faced with energy inflation seeping into the general market for goods and services, leading to overall inflation. Other issues do concern me, such as the effects which energy extraction, production, and usage have on the environment, but I leave that for another time and place.

The US has by far the largest oil deficit in the world, when measuring oil production versus consumption. China may soon overtake Japan for the number two position. Interestingly, countries like Japan, France, and Italy produce no oil at all, with France relying greatly on nuclear resources. Of note is that the few countries with the largest oil production deficits represent close to all of the world's GDP (although, if the price of oil continues to rise at a rapid rate, this will become further from the truth). In these countries' race to grow, each will have to increase its status as a net importer, unless each of them can increase its own level of oil production. As oil prices rise rapidly, so too will inflation, and the only way to prevent this inflation is to slow down the world-wide explosion in GDP growth, which can only be done through higher interest rates. It has become increasingly clear that this interest rate increase must be led by the Federal Reserve.

Just as with any supply-demand scenario, prices rise as the spread between the two narrow, and they explode when demand actually exceeds supply. If projections are for demand to continue exceeding supply, then prices will continue heading into record territory, and if projections are for demand to drop to levels below supply, then prices will slip to a more normal range. In the event projections are for demand to once again fall several percentage points below supply, then prices will fall significantly. Supply is subject to several potential bottlenecks, the two biggest being obtaining the crude and refining the crude. In the late 1990's and early 2000's, demand was slightly lower than refining capacity, but by late 2004, demand exceeded capacity. As any economist would expect, the result was skyrocketing oil prices.

To summarize, the world economy clearly does not run without oil. And when demand gets very close to or outstrips supply, the price of oil soars. And if these prices stay high, inflation rises. And if the Fed fears inflation, the Fed raises interest rates to slow down the world economy and reduce the demand for oil. If the reader understands this simplified relationship, then he/she understands much of the portion of economics that is actually proven.

Experts put the US in the middle of the pack in terms of oil used per unit of GDP. Not surprisingly, there are huge variations. Countries like Thailand, Indonesia, and China lead the pack in inefficiency, while Japan is the most efficient. Relative to the rest of the world, this puts the US in a pretty good position at first glance. But realizing that the US consumer buys its goods from inefficient countries, which will all experience inflation due to energy at some point, it becomes clear that the US is not so immune after all. When the cost of purchasing raw materials, running factories, and shipping finished goods are soaring due to runaway energy costs, it won't matter how low labor costs are, because this portion of the final cost will be dwarfed by all the energy dependent components.

The Real Cost of Gasoline

I heard an argument in the fall of 2005 that the average American was spending about 4% of his post-tax income on gasoline, far below the peak of 7% reached in the early 1980's. Optimists will attempt to use this information to convince the public that there is no inflation problem. Realists will see this number for what it truly is. I am a realist, and I believe the number is distorted. The major problem with such an argument is that the calculations include the most highly compensated, which pulls up average income. But these highly compensated individuals will hardly alter their fuel use. And the top earners make a far greater percentage of post-tax income today versus their percentage take in the early 1980's, so in order to arrive at a more meaningful comparison of spending on gasoline during the two periods of time, the numbers must be normalized. My calculations yield a normalized number of approximately 8% in mid-2005. This number tells me that the "typical" American's percent of post-tax income spent on gasoline may actually have been higher in 2005 than it was in the early 1980's. In addition, one needs to look at the effect that increasing health care costs are having on the "typical" wage earner in conjunction with energy costs, to more accurately gage the overall impact on the typical American. After delving into the details, the reader should see that this is simply yet another area where reported figures tell less than half the truth.

Crude Sweet Crude

Any graph of the price of crude reveals what has been occurring in the form of a classic bubble pattern. The Fed has two choices at this point. It can either pop the bubble now, or it can let the bubble run up some more, and then pop it at some point in the future. This latter rationale would be much like what Greenspan chose to do with the stock market bubble in the 1990's. Think of the pain which might have been averted had that bubble been popped sooner rather than later. If Bernanke stops raising interest rates prematurely and prices continue to rise, oil could reach $100 in 2006 or 2007. The US got lucky with natural gas, because the US had one its warmest winters on record, and much of the natural gas supply is used in the heating of homes. This can easily change, though. A good hurricane in the gulf, combined with a very cold winter, along with continued increases in the price of oil could act in unison to drive the prices of natural gas and oil to new heights.

Learn From History

History is a good friend when one is attempting to value any market. A forecaster can look at any combination of variables and/or events, and make projections which incorporate the current situation, to arrive at a likely scenario for the future. Let's review the history of oil crises, their effects on interest rates over a two-to-three-year-period, and their ultimate effects on the economy.

Oil Crisis	US Fed Funds Peak	Result
1973	13% in 1974 (up from 6%)	rates double and severe recession
1980	20% in 1981 (up from 6.5%)	rates triple and severe recession
2005	~5% in 2006 (up from 1%)	rates quintuple and?

While the numerical values of interest rates are still relatively low today when compared to past peaks, they are on their way to quintupling from their recent lows! These two prior recessions brought on by oil spikes only saw doubling and tripling of interest rates. Need I say more?

6

OTHER THINGS TO CONSIDER

Gold

Stocks are cyclical, the stock market is cyclical, the bond market is cyclical, interest rates are cyclical, inflation is cyclical, oil is cyclical, and now? Gold also has its own cycles. Gold's cycles might be tied to inflation, oil, deflation, instability, deficits, supply-demand, natural disasters and maybe even locusts. All these factors can act alone or together to drive gold up and down in short-term, medium-term, and long-term cycles. It's been said that one of gold's cycles is about 35 years in duration. One such possible gold cycle began in the late 1960's and bottomed out just a few years ago. Although gold never came down to near its levels of the previous bottom, normalized for inflation, it wasn't too far off. With gold on the rise again, it appears as though we may be in the midst of another 35-year cycle. Of course, there is no way of knowing whether it will fall short of, equal, or move ahead of the previous top, but if the cycle holds, the local top will be somewhere in a range, before gold begins its retreat once again.

Sometimes an investor can get a tip just listening to other people, provided he is in the right place at the right time. Such a thing happened to me. A couple of years ago I attended a Drexel University alumni event hosted by Steve Forbes. He told a small group of us that when gold is between 300 and 400, stocks do well, and when gold is outside this range, stocks do not do well. They do not necessarily do badly, but on average they do not do well. I do not know if he obtained this information from somewhere else or if he recognized the trend on his own. But now that I know of this believed relationship, I can look at historical patterns and see why it may be so. I do see problems with the relationship, as it could be just a strong coincidence which goes back to the beginning of the last gold cycle. Further, the theory may not factor inflation into the price range.

Whether a real correlation exists or not, the point is that if enough people believe something works, even if there is no rationale for its working (and that is not the case here), one needs to pay attention to it, because it can and will influence the markets. The question then becomes how strong that influence is relative to the hundreds of other variables that must be continuously factored into one's investment and trading models. And I must emphasize that if a man of Steve Forbes' stature believes that this trading range can influence the markets, this trading range does influence the markets.

Health Care

Ever since the federal government expanded Medicare benefits, there has been an increase in the number of businesses trimming or cutting healthcare benefits for retirees in various forms, beyond the changes which were already taking place prior to the enactment of the new rules. Current and future retirees will certainly be faced with large out-of-pocket expenses, and had better start saving now. Businesses are also continuing to offer health insurance to an ever-decreasing percentage of employees. These employees are also facing the reality of having to put aside more money to cover health care costs. Total health spending in the US is expected to come to about 20% of GDP by 2015. The actual numbers work out to about a 7% increase per year, based on figures from the Centers for Medicare and Medicaid Services. Whether the money comes from the government, from insurers, or out-of-pocket, clearly the money must come from somewhere, and that money is money which can no longer be spent on other things.

The Triple Play

US government figures show that today's total cost of Social Security, Medicare, and Medicaid is equal to approximately 8.5% of Gross Domestic Product. Projections are that by 2020, the total will be in the vicinity of 15%. Obviously, there must be significant change coming in the future to pay for all this. Perhaps qualifying ages will be moved up, perhaps benefits awarded will be cut in size and/or scope, and perhaps greater contributions will be expected from people who have earned and/or saved at various points in their lives. Nobody knows how things will turn out, but clearly there will be less government money available per capita in the future. And that means that if people expect to have the same level of income and services as today's retirees have, they had better start saving.

But people are not saving, as confirmed by the negative savings rate recorded in 2005 for the first time since the Great Depression. Sooner or later, change will have to come, and consumers will have to start saving. And when that change comes, people will cut back on spending, and when that happens, the economy will feel the pain.

7

TYING IT ALL TOGETHER

$200 Jeans

The $200 jeans are flying off the shelves. And they are flying off at huge profit margins. All this is happening while Costco sells a nicely cut, good looking pair of jeans for $12. I have tried many brands of jeans at places like GAP, Banana Republic, Bloomingdale's, Sak's, Urban Outfitters, American Eagle, and others. I've tried all these jeans, and I still haven't found the perfect jean (the right fit and the right look). So what's driving this frenzy? Strangely, maybe it's the real estate market.

And what does real estate have to do with jeans? It's called the "wealth effect", it came from the stock market in the late 1990's, and now it's coming from real estate. The difference is that now it's stronger than it was before, because 70% of households own their homes, whereas at the stock market peak, a far lesser percentage participated in that surge. Further, those who participated in the stock market gains of the late 90's tended to be better off, and their purchases of items like jeans were not so influenced by their market gains. Contrasted with the late 90's stock market, the beneficiaries of recent massive real estate gains include the majority of the middle class and a strong number of the less economically well off.

Naturally, parents want to make their kids happy, and they now have the means to give them the $200 jeans, the $100 sneakers, and the iPod, so that the kids can keep up with the "kid-Joneses". When the real estate market corrects and there are few people left to buy the $200 jeans, cash will be king, and many of these jeans will be had for a song and dance. At that time, the stocks of the companies which sell these jeans will follow in the footsteps of the kids of the parents who found themselves temporarily lifted to new heights by Greenspan's real estate bubble.

Follow the Money

Consumers get their spending money from several sources. One is from wages earned in their occupations. Others are from interest and dividends from savings and investments, and/or from inheritances. Yet another is from borrowing against the equity in their homes. As spending growth has overtaken income growth from the former sources, spenders (consumers) have chosen to take more and more equity from their homes as home values have risen. Recent results released by the Fed show borrowing against home equity as a share of disposable income increasing hyperbolically from about 1% in 1993 to 7% by 2004. This extraction of home equity alone has accounted for almost all of the recent gains in retail sales.

One might ask, what might happen if real estate values stop rising (I am not even addressing what happens if values fall). Let's assume real estate values remain locked in place, and homeowners decide not to borrow against the value of their homes because those values stopped rising. This will cause retail sales to be flat, which will cause stocks to drop, which will cause retail sales to fall (investors will feel less wealthy as home values flatten and their stock values fall), and on and on. This could, of course, then start a downward spiral in home prices a la Japan of the 1990's thru 2003. Chances are, however, our Fed learned some lessons from Japan, and would step in to prevent a full scale collapse as it did during the stock market crash of 2000-2003. Such actions, however, could set the stage for many years of stagnation and/or volatility in both the stock market and the real estate market.

Already, there are signs of a tapped-out consumer. The Federal Reserve reported that for 2005 consumer credit grew by only 3%, its slowest rate since 1992, which came in at 1%. And when consumer credit slows considerably, so too does the economy.

Many great sages are suggesting that business will pick up the reins when consumer spending grinds to a halt, but I question just how much money they will have to spend themselves. Businesses are staring at their own imposing triumvirate of pension funding, health care costs, and stock option expensing, and it is becoming increasingly difficult to see where they will get the necessary cash to pick up the slack left by the consumer.

Jeans and Gasoline

By 2006, average US demand for gasoline had stopped increasing and began decreasing. My interpretation of these events is that the US consumer has finally reached the breaking point. And as home prices stop rising (or start falling), while health care, tuition and energy costs continue their rapid paces of increase, the consumer will be forced to make some tough decisions. He has a negative savings rate for the first time since the Great Depression, and he will have to decide if he will go without health care so he can fill up his tank of gas and put food on the table. Maybe he will. But will he have his children go without health care so he can fill up his tank and drive to the mall to get the latest wide-screen flat-panel television and the $200 pair of jeans for all the kids? I doubt it. As oil prices rise, or even stay above $60, expect to see a consumer pullback in all areas of spending.

Even with the decrease in demand for gasoline, oil is likely to settle into a $40 to $50 price range, which represents about a 400% increase over its late 1990's lows. This is massive oil inflation, and it will affect the prices of everything. Only continued drastic measures by the Fed will pull the price down to levels below $40, and this will only be achieved in conjunction with a real estate and/or stock market correction.

Oil, Economics and Stock Markets

There is truly an amazing correlation between oil, the economy, and the stock market. There is strong evidence that the three US raging bull stock markets of the last century were all kicked off by similar forces. It appears as though an abrupt drop in oil prices from comparatively high levels conspired with a few other variables to take the stock market from cycle lows to cycle highs, although, naturally, it was the spike in oil prices which initially drove the markets down to cycle lows in the first place. In the most recent cycle, the 1980's saw falling interest rates as oil dropped 75% in real terms, and an accompanying economic and stock market boom. By 1999, oil had briefly plunged to the low-teens, perhaps a new all-time low. Is it any wonder that the economy and stock markets soared to unimaginable levels by early 2000?

Following the market crash of 2000 and fearing a potential repeat of the Great Depression, Greenspan opened the money spigots, and in the process drove oil to its present levels. I think it's safe to say that Greenspan avoided a repeat of the 1930's (for the time being at least), but while the economy and stock market took advantage of the still relatively low cost of oil through 2004, by 2005 we were back in 1970's territory. Given where we are on the oil front, we can look forward to ever-increasing interest rates until the price of oil comes back down to a much lower level than where it is today. Until we get there, we can forget about stock market booms.

Inflation and Real Estate

Comparing rates of inflation and rates of home price increases has been an industry guide to valuations for nearly as long as anyone can remember. This is because one of the primary reasons for purchasing a home has traditionally been as a hedge against inflation. The thinking then follows that real estate values should out-perform inflation by about 1% to 2% per year to account for some of the cost of home maintenance and real estate taxes. This relationship held up fairly well from 1976 thru 1995, but real estate pulled ahead dramatically in the 1996 to 2000 period, only to completely dwarf the rate of inflation since 2001. Of note is that even if we use "real inflation" numbers rather than the Fed's stated inflation rates of recent years, the recent cycle of real estate out-performance would still be extreme.

Assets and GNP

The "wealth effect" is something that has affected the behavior of markets since the beginning of time. The wealth effect is in a sense a self-fulfilling prophesy, and is a simple concept to understand. So simple, in fact, that it is often overlooked. Here is how it works. When asset values are rising, people who own those assets feel wealthier. Since those people didn't have to labor to earn that extra wealth, they generally feel as though it was a gift to them. They generally treat that gift as spending money, and they go out for a good time. This increased spending acts to drive up the value of any market which receives the benefits of that additional spending. This market can be the stock market, the real estate market, and/or other markets. When the value of any or all of these markets has been driven to an unsustainable level, the party comes to an end. The "reverse wealth effect" then kicks into gear. As market values fall, people feel less wealthy (maybe even poor), and they stop spending. This causes valuations of market(s) to fall even more. This spiral goes 'round and 'round, generally until valuations have overshot to the down side. This is precisely the time to buy into those markets, provided that one has cash available.

In 2005, US net household wealth moved above its 2000 highs for the first time. As this number continues to grow beyond the $50 trillion mark, up more than two-fold since the mid-1980's, we find ourselves in a precarious situation. Since I believe the US is experiencing a real estate bubble and a stock market echo bubble, I feel this number will have to fall considerably sometime in the near future. The ratio of household wealth to GDP in the US is approximately one-third higher in 2006 than it was in the mid-1990's, yet my expectation is that this ratio should be a steady value, because the ratio already reflects the contribution from its components. What I mean by this is that the "wealth effect" generated by increasing household wealth helps to increase GDP, and therefore is already reflected in rising GDP numbers. Inasmuch, the ratio should remain fairly constant regardless of whether GDP is rising or falling. At most, I would expect slight increases or decreases in the ratio to reflect the direction of GDP growth (or shrinkage), and to account for euphoria or depression on the part of market participants. Clearly, there is something very euphoric occurring, much as there was in early 2000. Perhaps part of the explanation is that Americans are saving less and putting a greater percentage of their money into stock and real estate investments, thereby driving the ratio higher. In the event the ratio got back to mid-1990's levels in a very short timeframe, household wealth could lose about one-third of its early 2006 value. Further, there is no guarantee that the mid-1990's represents a "floor", as by some measures, the stock market was overvalued at that time. Finally, at that time, the economy was still operating in an environment of long-term decreasing interest rates, whereas it may have now entered a period of long-term increasing interest rates, which could have very harmful effects on valuations of both the stock market and the real estate market.

Household Debt-to-Income Ratio

Numbers from the Federal Reserve show that the household debt-to-income ratio was up from less than 0.9 in 1994 to 1.2 in 2004. That translates to a move of about 33% in a ten-year period, and it's been growing on an exponential path in the most recent years. One thing everybody should know by now is that when it comes to the investment markets, almost all exponential and hyperbolic trends correct. Sometimes they correct 20 or 25% and flatten out, and other times they come crashing down as much as 90% or more, in the case of certain individual stocks or hyper-growth market sectors. It is extremely unlikely that the debt-to-income ratio will fall 90%, as it is unlikely it would even fall 50% (the Fed and the government would intervene to prevent this), but a 25% drop back to 0.9 is not out of the question.

What could cause this drop?

Perhaps the government will impose stricter mortgage lending rules to prevent an even greater real estate bubble than the one which exists, or maybe the Fed will rapidly raise interest rates to deal with inflation. Either way, the result would be a pull-back in housing prices, and as fear replaces greed, a spiral of fewer buyers, more sellers, falling prices, and fewer people taking on new debt would be set in motion. This would spill over into consumer spending, as people would suddenly choose to pay off their debts rather than spend on goods financed with more debt. Even the new bankruptcy laws enacted in 2005 would contribute to this effect, as people would increasingly fear the possibility of being unable to shed their debt. Bankruptcies surged just prior to the new law going into effect, and following the new bankruptcy rules, fewer people will be taking on more debt to finance conspicuous consumption. Higher interest rates will also result in a serious cutback on debt loads. The past two years have seen a relatively large jump in the rates of variable home equity lines of credit and credit cards. This is representative of a changing environment in which debt will become ever more costly. All these things together (along with any stock market correction, higher energy prices, and/or inflation) will curb the consumer's appetite to spend and therefore to take on more debt, resulting in a correction to the household debt-to-income ratio. This correction will be healthy for the markets in the long term, but there will be short-term consequences.

Estimates are that by the end of 2005, consumers had a net savings deficit of over $500 billion. Now that it is a forgone conclusion that the real estate boom has ended, where will people get their spending money from?

Bank Risks

The FDIC loan loss reserve ratio is at two-decade lows, the consumer is completely tapped out and completely reliant on continued home price appreciation, and by some estimates, mortgage-related debt is at over half of total bank credit. Contrary to popular belief that bank risks have been hedged away through collateralized mortgage obligations, those banks will likely take massive hits when the real estate bubble implodes. One can only wonder what might happen to the rest of the economy and to the stock market should this occur, and one can only wonder why the government is not increasing these loss reserves.

Real Estate and the Economy

Studies have shown that housing price declines typically lead to greater economic damage and leave an economy weaker for a longer period of time than do stock market declines. Very often, the damage is so severe that the real estate decline pulls the stock market down along with it. One needs to look no further than recent Japanese history for confirmation of the devastating effects which overvalued markets can have on themselves. The reason for this is tied to the "reverse wealth effect".

The wealth effect prompted US households to use home equity lending to obtain funds to spend the equivalent of perhaps as much as 3% of GNP in 2005. If home prices were to fall, homeowners would pull back, and this endless supply of money for the economy would dry up over night. The 3 or 4% growth in GNP might abruptly fall to 1 or 2% as a result of a stagnant real estate market. But it gets worse, because the housing sector by some estimates accounts for up to 35% of total US economic activity. How's this?

Construction alone accounts for about 5% of GNP, and adding real estate brokerage, banking, mortgage lending, consumer finance, insurance, much of the consumer durables sector, home services, and other related businesses, quickly brings the total to the 35% range. All would be deeply affected by a correction in housing prices, and the ensuing ripple effect would work its way throughout the entire economy. It should be noted that the scenario we examined is for a stagnant real estate market. Should valuations decline, the result could be anything from recession to depression.

Trouble in Paradise

Reports are appearing that the Manhattan real estate market has finally cracked. Most people expected it would be at the lower end first (studios and less desirable one-bedrooms), and affect the kind of properties that only newcomers would buy at such elevated prices. To some degree this type of thinking makes sense. Buyers of such properties would scrape together whatever they could for a meager down payment before a home became completely unaffordable to them. They could get an interest-only no-money down, adjustable-low-doc mortgage, or some other hybrid of gobbledygook.

On the other hand, people buying those expensive 2- and 3-bedrooms have plenty of money, and many of them technically could afford to buy several such places if they so desired. Or so I keep hearing from people who believe they understand the investment markets. The reality is that there are relatively few people who can afford the higher-end residences in Manhattan. Consider that so many of these types of places have been built or converted, that supply has finally outrun demand at super high price points. Even if there were many people left who both wanted and could afford these homes, many of theses people are very business savvy and can recognize when a market is highly overvalued (recall from an earlier chapter that the rich have been cutting back on their real estate investment allocation). For these reasons, the correction has begun to form at the top end of the market rather than at the bottom. I believe now that lending standards have finally begun tightening, the correction will next show itself on the low end. It should then continue to work its way down from the top and up from the bottom, until those in the middle are squeezed (more attractive one-bedrooms and less exclusive two-bedrooms). At that point, the correction will be in full force and there will be nowhere to hide. Each local market may behave in its own way, but more or less, other markets will follow patterns similar to that of Manhattan.

No More Saving, No More Growth

Commerce Department numbers showed that the personal savings rate fell to minus 0.7% in December, to finish all of 2005 at negative 0.5%. The US now has a negative savings rate, a feat not accomplished since 1933! The rapid decline in the savings rate, which came down from 3% in mid-2003, has coincided with a rapid escalation in home price appreciation. This suggests that consumers no longer believe in saving because home appreciation is doing the saving for them, or that they no longer are able to save because their wages have not kept up with rising expenses. Sadly, either scenario has a dark ending. Now that home prices have stopped appreciating, consumers will be forced to save more money, resulting in decreasing fortunes and stock prices for the retailers, which will spill over to the rest of the stock market. To substantiate my reasoning, there have been numerous studies showing that a pull-back in consumer spending of only a few percentage points can result in a very significant recession.

Looked at another way, assuming a savings rate of zero, the typical consumer relies primarily on home price appreciation for his/her savings. But the homeowner must also factor in the cost of carrying a home. Estimates in the current environment put carrying costs at about 5 to 10%, which means home prices must appreciate at least this much per year for the typical homeowner to come out ahead. Should home price appreciation turn into depreciation, this would create an extremely challenging environment (in fairness, one must also weigh the benefits of not having to pay rent for a home). It is important to note that this exercise did not even address the detrimental effects of inflation.

Global Interest Rates

We are in the midst of an anomaly. Central bankers around the world have engaged in targeting inflation in recent decades, generally resulting in short-term rates averaging about 2 to 3 percentage points above the level of stated inflation. This worked effectively through the 1980's and 1990's, but with the collapse of global stock markets in 2000, everything changed. Led by Greenspan, rates were lowered around the globe in an effort to avoid deflation and to spur growth. For about three years, short-term rates hovered at the level of reported inflation (in reality they were something less than inflation), and only in the last two years (since 2004) have they come off their lows. If modern history is any guide, rates will continue rising until they arrive at the magic level of stated inflation plus 2.5%, which implies they could be at 6 % by mid-2006.

Add It Up

By the end of 2005, a situation existed in which the consumer was being squeezed in almost every possible way. Interest rates were rising (which will likely drive down the value of consumers' homes), health care costs were going up much faster than wage growth (and more of these costs were being shifted to the consumer), energy costs had already exploded and will remain high, personal bankruptcy laws became more restrictive, real inflation was considerably higher than the government stated inflation rate, the AMT (Alternative Minimum Tax) was threatening an ever-increasing number of middle-class taxpayers, and jobs were still being outsourced at an alarming rate.

As interest rates rise and the rate of home price appreciation slows, or even reverses to depreciation, projections are that consumer mortgage equity withdrawals will slow considerably. One Wall Street firm is forecasting a drop-off of about 30% from the highs of 2005, translating into several hundred billions of dollars over the course of the three years. While the effect this will have on the economy is open to debate, what is clear is that it will have a substantial effect. What's worse is that it could contribute to what could become a vicious cycle of less spending and more home price depreciation, along with possible effects on the stock market. What I am suggesting is that we are truly entering the world of the unknown, and this world demands extreme caution!

Bankruptcy

My, how times in the US have changed. Back in the old days (earlier 20th century), when there was a very small government support network (or none), people did not declare bankruptcy. There are many reasons for this, but let's not dwell on those reasons when today's numbers make the US look like a nation of gamblers. Even in the midst of the Great Depression, bankruptcies were virtually unheard of. In 1978, Congress liberalized the bankruptcy laws.

There's an old saying that goes "you give a man enough rope and he hangs himself", and in this case it couldn't be truer. Since 1978, the number of personal bankruptcies had surged to over 500 per 100,000 people per year. Just to put things in perspective, this means that at its peak, each year about 1% of households had been declaring bankruptcy. Many of them may have done so more than once over the decades. Clearly, the era of shame and self-respect is over.

Some economists and academics give special reasons for the high numbers of bankruptcies, and portray all the victims as helpless. They generally claim that almost all the reasons for the bankruptcies are due to loss of employment, medical problems, or divorce, which could give the impression that nobody is responsible for their own failure to plan and save. Obviously, many people who declare bankruptcy have been hit by great misfortune, and the option of bankruptcy should always be made available to them, but the reality is that many others are simply lazy in their work habits, irresponsible with their saving and investing, and/or thoughtless in their spending. The US has always had a host of problems its citizens had to deal with, but historically bankruptcy rates were much lower.

But then again, if the government has made it so easy to file for and to emerge from bankruptcy, what should one expect? What the government created was a moral hazard. Consider the man who has saved little, and decides that he will not attempt to save any more. After all, at some point he can rely on Medicaid, Medicare, and Social Security to take care of him. He ponders why he should bother saving ten, twenty, or fifty thousand dollars at the expense of enjoying what little he has. On the other hand, if he can get a big payoff, he could be set for life. So why not play the lottery every day, or go to Las Vegas and hope to get lucky, or put all his money on that internet stock option. After all, if he losses, so his thinking goes, the government will be there to take care of him. Of course, in the meantime, while he is busy spending his money and not bothering to save for the proverbial "rainy day", he is diagnosed with a heart condition. He may never be able to afford to cover his medical bills (even if he has insurance) because he has spent all his money, and his inevitable bankruptcy gets chalked up to a "medical problem". Hopefully everyone can see the absurdity in tabulating the "reasons" for bankruptcy.

Of course, employees of the credit-card issuers, the Wall Street firms and the casinos (and let's not forget the lottery organizations), have been trained to recognize potential "customers". And they are ready to take their customers' money in a multitude of ways. And they will always have a great opportunity for their customers, no matter the investment environment. And should a customer find an advisor who recommends that their customer hold all his/her money in high-yielding, safe money-market funds, chances are that advisor will not be around for very long, because this will not generate the necessary fees to justify that advisor's wages.

The beauty of the entire system is that those who would take people's money don't have to feel very guilty. This is precisely because the government has provided all sorts of safety nets in the form of starting over (bankruptcy), Medicare, Medicaid and Social Security. And therein lies the moral hazard. It is a system in which conservative taxpayers and savers (sadly, these responsible citizens often find themselves the subject of ridicule for being risk-averse and are often called "cheapskates" when they refuse to blow their money on frivolous things) fund the risky lifestyles of reckless people, while predators walk away with bucket loads of money.

Proprietary Trading

Many of the more well-capitalized pros incorporate their data into elaborate computer trading programs. The "Big Board" reported that "program" trading accounted for 57% of NYSE volume in 2005. This builds on the rapid increases over the last several years, and puts the less knowledgeable and less experienced investor at an even greater disadvantage than in prior times.

A good number of these pros are "shorting" the markets, and even the QQQQ (Nasdaq 100 Index ETF) may have had almost half its shares shorted at one point in 2005. The power of the shorts is one of many forces which caused the markets to gyrate over 5% up and down, several times in 2004 and 2005. What's most interesting about this is that many Wall Street firms make a considerable portion of their profits from proprietary trading, yet their analysts, economists, and advisors tell their customers to hold the usual blend of stocks, bonds, and cash for the long term. The reader should recall from the earlier section of the book concerning myths that traders will use the public's long-term money as "ballast".

At this juncture, the reader should be thinking that this all really does not make much sense. After all, if the firms make most of their money from trading, perhaps they should be telling him to trade the same financial instruments which they are trading (they can't for various reasons). And if the firms are telling him to buy and hold, then they should be buying and holding as well. But what a beautiful business it is, where they can tell him, the less informed investor to do one thing, while they do another.

The pros make money every way. They make it on proprietary trading, and they make it on fees. And they make it when the investor acts on their advice, and they make it when he doesn't. The investor must understand that the game is "rigged". It is not "rigged" in the sense that the pros will steal from him, but rather, in the sense that there are so many aspects to their businesses, that there will always be ways for them to come out ahead at his expense. It is, in fact, a zero-sum game, and the small investor is almost always the loser.

"Conundrum"

Much has been made of Greenspan's speech in which he used the word "conundrum" to describe the situation in which long-term interest rates are not responding to short-term rate increases. I have plenty of ideas why this is so, but was curious to see exactly what Greenspan meant by his use of the word. So I went to The American Heritage Dictionary and found the following definitions for "conundrum":

1. A riddle in which a fanciful question is answered by a pun.

2. A problem admitting of no satisfactory solution.

3. A difficult and complicated problem.

These three definitions suggest very different meanings of the word "conundrum", so it is very important to try to narrow down which of these Greenspan intended to convey at the time he made his statement. It is my personal belief that Greenspan did not intend for us to use the first definition, but rather a combination of the second and third. I believe that the third definition is inferred by the second inasmuch that a problem with no satisfactory solution is a difficult and complicated problem. So let's take the third definition as a given, and focus on the second. Let's further focus on "no satisfactory solution".

I believe that there was, and is a solution to the problem.

The solution is that the government should get more involved, and force a tightening of lending standards on mortgages. The problem with this solution is that the government waited until very late in the game to get involved. The reasons for the government not wanting to tighten standards are myriad. One such reason is that the US economy is a free market economy, and government interference would be nothing less than admitting that the US needs to back track from a totally free capitalist economic model. But perhaps the stronger reason for not wanting to interfere with lending standards was the knowledge that if and when this occurred, there would be major fallout. Real estate price appreciation would slow, or fall to depreciation, consumer spending would slow or fall, and stock markets and real estate values would drop, precipitating a vicious cycle. Nobody wants this to occur, except perhaps the "bears" (those betting that one or more asset classes will fall) and traders, so Greenspan and company just inched along with quarter point increases, hoping that things would slowly take care of themselves. Unfortunately for Greenspan, the problem with this approach is that we've seen it before (think stock market, 1999). Ultimately, the boiling point is reached, and small cracks turn into gaping holes.

Now that we understand how the problem should have been solved (through government regulation and higher interest rates) earlier in the game, we need to focus on why this solution is not (no longer) satisfactory. Consumers lost a lot of money in the stock market crash a few years ago, and home ownership has in many cases become those consumers' sole savings vehicles, and even their lenders of last resort. Woe to the person (and administration) that takes away the punch bowl (the real estate bubble) from this party. Should the bubble pop, a majority of consumers would have little money to spend and consumer confidence would plummet. This would not have a very good effect on the war effort in Iraq, as the public would demand that funds spent on the Iraq campaign (and on defense in general) be curtailed or greatly reduced, and brought home. Similarly, focus would shift to the large-scale tax cuts granted to the super-rich at the expense of the middle class and the "not-as-rich". Now we have a larger picture of the true conundrum, or in other words, "a difficult and complicated problem, which admits of no satisfactory solution, and presents itself as a riddle, just begging to be answered by a pun".

More on "Conundrum"

I love that word. I love it so much so that I can't stop writing about it.

I believe that Greenspan said there was a conundrum because he couldn't (didn't want to) tell the public what was really going on. Some great words of wisdom came from a co-worker of mine in 1989 while we were designing one of the most advanced aircraft engines in the world. He was a brilliant engineer. He was still earning an engineer's salary while many of his contemporaries were entering their peak earning years at far higher compensation levels, in far less challenging jobs in other industries. He conveyed to me the lesson he had learned from others. He said to "make as much money as you can, as fast as you can". I never fully embraced this idea personally (as I doubt he did), but it did contribute to my departure from engineering. I tell this story to help you understand what is going on with this "conundrum", which is not really a conundrum.

Banks, mortgage lenders, builders, other companies, foreign governments (China), and all the other stakeholders in the game have the same interest. They wish to "make as much money as they can, as fast as they can", and they can only do this if interest rates are low. This has lead the finance companies (including companies with large finance arms) to do whatever they can to keep the party going by creating easier ways for consumers to get credit and mortgages. It has lead the Chinese government (and others) to purchase US government securities to keep rates low, which in turn will keep the US housing bubble growing, which will, in turn, keep the US consumer spending, which will keep the Chinese (emerging) economy growing. Public companies not involved in the business of financing share the goal of low interest rates, as those low interest rates enable consumers and businesses to purchase more of their products, resulting in growing revenues, profits and stock prices.

But, as stock prices (and home values) rise, the pros are heading for the exits. I wrote earlier that the wealthy had already reduced their allocation to real estate from 2003 to 2004. For the past two years, corporate insiders have been selling stock at rates relative to their purchases at record levels. This ratio has never been so high for so long, and it shows that in just about every industry, insiders are cashing out. It mirrors what is happening in the real estate market. The great news for the insiders is that they are making "as much money as they can, as fast as they can", and when their stocks fall (and many may go out of business), they will have already gotten out with a great deal of their money. The small, unsophisticated shareholder will be left, however, holding the bag.

Real Estate and Stocks

There are all sorts of debates over relationships between the housing market and the stock market, and the effects of corrections and crashes. Hyper-valued housing markets on the coasts are sometimes compared to internet stocks, tech stocks, and Dow stocks. I see these markets as being most similar to the Dow and the S&P500 in early 2000. The ensuing correction took the Dow down about 40% and the S&P about 50%. Because the hyper-valued real estate markets comprise an ever-larger proportion of the total US real estate market, even if the average value of a home outside of these markets rises, average and median US prices will likely fall for the first time in recent history (the drop will be far greater in real terms). This is because the extent of over-valuation in the hyper-valued markets will drag the aggregate numbers down. Further, the most insanely overpriced local real estate markets that are totally dominated by the new hybrid and low doc, no doc type loans, very well may experience Nasdaq, 2000-like crashes.

Of great concern is the myth that home values cannot collapse as quickly as stocks can. With home ownership rates at a high, values stretched further than ever, record numbers of second and third home owners, record numbers of investors in the market, the lowest interest rates in 40 years, and extreme "margin", all the ingredients are in place for a very rapid decline in prices. And the reason most often sited to make the argument that this cannot happen is bogus. Whether people sell fast or slowly, prices move to where they want to be at a given time. Recall that the stock market went from a high in March, 2000 to a low in October, 2002. That move took two and one-half years. The stock market crash in October, 1987 took two days. The same can happen with real estate. If nobody wants to buy, then prices fall, and they can fall with a vengeance. It could take one week, one month, one year, or 10 years. Nobody knows!

Another myth is that stocks move as a single market and homes do not. This could have been remotely true for homes in the past, when local bubbles formed as a result of surging local economies. But that is not the case this time. This time almost all local markets have been soaring simply due to the availability of easy money and changes in capital gains tax policy. And recall that, if nothing else, we learned in 2000 that stocks don't move as a single market either. The Nasdaq plunged by a far greater percentage and earlier than did the Dow. The wise among us took the signal from the Nasdaq and sold the Dow, before its great plunge began. So too, certain hyper-valued real estate markets will likely crack prior to the rest, and serve as an early warning system for investors in those other markets. It's true that all the local markets won't fall at the same exact time, but once a few of them fall, they will all fall.

The Ingredients

It appears that the necessary ingredients for a correction have finally arrived. Interest rates are clearly on their way up, and although they could come back down a little, it is unlikely they will approach their recent lows for another generation. The Fed finally started jaw-boning lenders, which doled out mortgages the way my neighbor gave candy to trick-or-treaters with huge appetites on Halloween. And tax cut talk has turned to tax break cuts when it comes to mortgage interest rate deductibility. This triumvirate is exactly what all the bears have been waiting for, and going forward each price drop is likely to precipitate more price drops, and each default is likely to precipitate more defaults, until the cycle bottoms.

Uncharted Territory

There have always been unknowns in life, and there always will be. We have lessons from Greek mythology (so we should be able to recognize "myths" by now), the Bible, and today, nature and science to continuously remind us that life is full of surprises.

On the heels of the lowest interest rates in over 40 years, along with steep tax cuts for everything from earned and unearned income to residential real estate gains, the US economy now finds itself with a housing bubble and a stock market echo bubble, a negative personal savings rate, and the largest twin deficits in recent history.

The Fed has precedent for popping bubbles. The stock market bubble of 1929 was popped by the Fed's rapid interest rate increases, resulting in a deflationary depression, in which the stock market would not get back to its prior level for 24 years. The Japanese bubble of 1989 was popped by the Fed's Japanese equivalent, resulting in deflationary stagnation, leaving the Nikkei down over 80% by 2003. The US mini-bubble of the 1960's was done in by a slew of factors including rising oil prices, war, union activity, falling productivity, inflation, and foreign competition (Japan), as the Fed raised rates. The Fed attempted to jawbone the US stock market bubble of the 1990's with Greenspan's famous "irrational exuberance" speech in 1996, but the markets saw he couldn't be too serious when he promptly lowered rates to save Long Term Capital Management and the financial industry. By late 1999 he had no choice, and became intent on popping the bubble. After raising rates to pop that bubble, the Fed was well aware of the damage that would be inflicted on the world as markets tumbled, so it began lowering rates rapidly, and then held them there for a couple of years, to prevent a repeat of the 1930's in the US or the 1990's in Japan.

As it turned out, the Fed has succeeded, but at what cost? Now there is an even larger total asset bubble than there was in 2000, but this time it comes with rising twin deficits, war, rising oil prices, increasing foreign competition, homeland security financial obligations and a host of other problems. Does this sound like a time that US assets should be at a high in relation to its GNP? It doesn't to me, but since it is, it suggests to me that in the short term, US asset values will fall significantly.

The Three Rules

The three rules of real estate are not only the three rules of real estate, but are the three rules of the investment markets. "Location, location, location" matters in the real estate market, as does individual stock selection (the "location, location, location" of the stock market) in the stock market. But what matters more than location, location, location in either the stock market or the real estate market is "cycle, cycle, cycle". Just as there is a cycle in real estate, there are cycles in equities, bonds, gold, oil, collectibles, and commodities. There are even cycles in the fashion industry. You name something, and it has a cycle.

The larger equity and bond market cycles tend to move with interest rates, but there are lots of intermediate- and short-term cycles, right down to the seasons (as it says in the Bible and in the Byrds' song). As it has always been, the best way to make money is to buy at the right time (the low point in the cycle) and to sell at the right time (the high point in the cycle). Do the opposite, and location doesn't mean nearly as much as the experts would have one believe. When the market goes up, almost everything goes up, and when the market goes down, almost everything goes down, or as the old Wall Street saying goes: "a rising tide lifts all ships". Just don't expect your financial advisor or your real estate broker to tell you what happens when the tide falls.

My Projection

The Fed will come to the rescue, guiding the world real estate and stock markets to a soft landing, peace will break out among the nations, debt will "evaporate", and then I wake up. If only real life was just a bad dream.

My projection for the most likely short- to medium-term scenario for the investment markets is that the Fed will continue increasing interest rates to pop the real estate bubble and stamp out inflation. Housing prices will fall in local bubble markets and probably nationally as well, certainly in real terms. Consumers who have little savings will cut back on spending. Stock prices will fall and imports from China and other low-cost markets will slow. Those nations will purchase fewer US Treasuries, allowing long-term rates to rise. These rising rates will make homes even less affordable, causing prices of homes to fall further, and causing the entire cycle to repeat in a downward spiral until some equilibrium point is reached. Most likely, that point will be reached several months after the Fed is through raising rates and has embarked on a new cycle of easing. By that time, the stock market will have taken a big hit due to the reverse wealth effect's impact on the economy. It is impossible to accurately forecast the magnitude of the dual correction (stock and real estate markets) because too much depends on how the many interacting variables play out over the course of time. The magnitudes of the corrections are therefore moving targets, but it would not be unreasonable to assume that the US real estate market and the stock market each could fall by as much as 25% or more in real terms. The stock market would likely bounce back, and fluctuate in a manner similar to that experienced in the 1970's, while the real estate market would remain in the doldrums for several years before entering its next growth cycle.

The economies, interest rates, and by extension, real estate markets of the world have become so intertwined in the last decade that they will likely all move essentially in lock step, probably with a few months lag between countries, and a slight lag between each country's stock market and real estate market. So as the downward spiral moves along its steady course, it will suck down the real estate markets, economies, and stock markets of the world, until the Fed has had enough. At that point, the Fed will embark on an interest rate lowering journey, and in time the investment markets will begin their recoveries.

Savvy traders will have many opportunities to make a great deal of money on the way down, just as they were able to do so when the stock market crashed a few years ago. As the markets finally recover, the savvy trader and the industry insiders will be ready and waiting once again.

8

EPILOGUE

Surfing and Trading

For the investor who wants to truly learn how to invest, I recommend watching the surfers. Spend a few days studying techniques employed by the best surfers in the world. The best surfers may or may not realize it, but they are honing skills that every successful investor who hopes to compete with the pros needs to possess. I initially made this observation many years ago as I sat and marveled at the skill of the surfers. As I contemplated their actions, I couldn't help but notice the similarities between surfing and trading stocks. Watch the great surfers. Observe their patience. They will sit for hours at a time on their boards amidst the waves, waiting, studying the waves, and observing. Sometimes they might make just a couple of runs in an entire day. What are they doing? They are observing patterns.

The great surfers watch the wave height, the wavelength, the momentum, other surfers, and many other variables. They are preparing themselves so that they are ready for the best wave of the day, and so that they will be able to identify it before it arrives, catch it as it builds in height and energy, and ultimately ride it in as it breaks and comes into the shoreline. They are also conserving their energy (energy is the surfer's basic resource as cash is the investor's basic resource) so that they can take full advantage when the great wave comes along. While awaiting the perfect wave, they may miss a few good ones, but they will also miss the far more numerous lousy waves which give false "ride" ("buy") signals. The greatest surfers are extremely adept at picking the best wave, and then riding it for as long as that wave is useful to them.

In the investing world, the surfing analogy would equate to buying the best asset (or stock) before or as it is picking up its momentum, riding it to the top, and then either getting out at the top and going to cash, or going short at the top, and then making money all the way down. "Long-only's" would just ride the wave to the top and then go to cash. "Short-only's" would start shorting at the top and ride the wave in. The "long-shorts" would do both.

Some surfers will catch a wave (buy a stock position), decide they made an error, and shortly thereafter, get off the wave ("cutting their losses"). In the process, they position themselves for the next wave (next stock or cycle) to come along. My "surfing" method applies to individual stocks, industry sectors, and even entire markets. It can also be used with real estate, bonds, currency, commodities, art, and anything else which exhibits wavelike (cycle) activity.

Storms, Tsunami's, and Other Lessons from Nature

Many market analysts, including the Elliott Wave theorists often use Fibonacci curves to help them predict market movements. It has been observed that there are naturally occurring patterns in nature that repeat themselves. One such set of patterns are those on the nautilus shell. A similar pattern appears in the photos of the galaxy of stars in the universe. Analysts observed similar curves in stock market patterns, particularly when applied to stock indexes. They have since described these patterns with mathematical formulas and have attempted (sometimes with great accuracy) to predict ensuing market movements.

I have found that there are numerous lessons found in the patterns of nature which can be applied to the investment markets, and can therefore make everyone better investors.

These investing lessons come directly from Mother Nature. The first is concerning storms. Storms in general can come with or without warning, but there is a phrase which the investor can learn a lot from, which is "the calm before the storm". This phrase caught on for good reason. People least expect a storm when the sky is blue, there is no wind, it's comfortable, and there is not a worry or concern. But everyone has learned from repeated experience that this is often the most dangerous time. It is so dangerous precisely because we become complacent, we let out guards down, and then, before we know it, the sky turns gray, the wind picks up, the rain begins to fall, and we are stranded someplace far from home and unprepared. It could be a brief thunder shower or snow shower, or it could be something far more severe, like a major hurricane, earthquake, volcano, or tsunami. Thankfully, these days we are forewarned by our local weatherpeople, who receive the most up-to-date information from satellites circling the earth. But even satellites and other devices can't catch them all (like tornadoes that appear out of nowhere causing swift and complete devastation, and earthquakes and tsunamis which can give very little warning).

We can use this information which Mother Nature has bestowed upon us to our advantage when it comes to investing. Stock market volatility indexes (VIX and VXN) speak volumes about where we are on the relative scale of market volatility. The curves are near their historic lows in early 2006, telling us there is great complacency in the markets. This is "the calm before the storm". It is the time you do not want to wander off far from home without your raincoat and a supply of food. You should be hunkering down, getting ready for the storm which will follow the calm, because it is on its way. Furthermore, there are some insightful weatherpeople out there warning you about the impending storm, but your TV is tuned to the wrong channel (you may be watching Cramer or another entertaining show). When the storm hits, there will be a jump in the volatility index. Its sudden jump will actually resemble the jumps produced by earthquake monitoring systems utilizing the Richter system. Depending on the severity of this storm or earthquake, the jump in the index could be slight or huge, and it can come back down quickly, or remain elevated for some time. It can oscillate up and down over a period of time before once again settling back down into a temporarily calm state prior to the next eruption. As in nature (with storms, hurricanes, earthquakes, and volcanoes) we don't always know how severe the next eruption will be, but we do know that the greater the pressure buildup (i.e. bubbles), the greater the eruption will be (when the bubble pops). It's important to understand that the investment markets, which we reduce to and represent by a series of graphs are another form of natural phenomena created by the mass psychology of man (which taken together is another large force of nature).

One of the greatest lessons all investors should have learned came in the form of 2004's Tsunami. I was heart-broken for the victims of this disaster, but I was also fascinated by the event. I wanted to learn as much about this Tsunami as I could.

Let's look at what causes this type of Tsunami to occur. One tectonic plate is sliding under a second plate. As the first plate slides under, frictional forces pull the second plate down with it. At some point in time, the fictional forces are overwhelmed, and the second plate pops up. This creates the devastating swell of water that rises up and then radiates out from that area (fault line). I see a definite parallel between the image of the slopes of the tectonic plates and the conundrum Greenspan spoke of with regard to the yield curve.

Even though the Fed is aggressively pushing up short-term rates as it attempts to get long-term rates up, there are many market forces conspiring to hold long-term rates down. Using the Tsunami analogy, the market forces are the frictional forces between the plates which are keeping them locked in place despite the pressure buildup. As the Fed pushes up rates and the opposing forces push down to try to resist, more and more pressure builds. A point in time will finally come when the forces of increasing short-term rates will be so powerful (we will likely have an inverted yield curve at this point) that they will finally overpower the resisting forces, and cause an explosive upward move in long-term rates. (This would be analogous to when the tectonic plate on top snaps upward, creating the water swell, resulting in the Tsunami). Such a powerful and rapid move up in interest rates would have a ripple effect throughout the financial markets of the world. The level to which the Fed has to take short-term rates before this snap occurs will determine the magnitude of the explosion in long-term rates. They could conceivably jump a couple of percentage points in a very short timeframe. Such a move could cause real estate, stock, and bond markets to undergo significant corrections, possibly crashes, which in the long term could cause even more human suffering than the Tsunami of 2004.

I don't wish to create a panic. I just want readers to be aware of the parallels between the forces of nature and the forces guiding the behavior of the investment markets. I believe everyone should lighten up on their real estate and stock holdings and be invested primarily in short-term government securities until the investment climate changes significantly.

Odds, Spreads, and Ratios

Many people place bets on sporting events, so I dedicate this exercise to all the gamblers out there who have honed their skills and utilize mathematical techniques available to them in their quest for victory in the field.

Bets are rarely "even money" in the gambling world. Almost always, one competitor is favored to win. To level the playing field, gamblers utilize "odds" and "spreads". In sports like boxing and horse racing, the method employed is "odds". A fighter might be a two-to-one or a three-to-two favorite over his competitor. Generally in high scoring sports like basketball and football, "spreads" take over. A heavily favored team may have to subdue its opponent by more than 6 points to actually win the bet ("beat the spread"). Exactly what determines whether the sport is more suited for "odds" or a "spread" is best left for another discussion, but the goal in each case is to level the playing field, so that either side of the bet has an approximately equal chance of winning. Of course, the bookie always takes his cut, ensuring a stream of income to himself, which rises with the volume of bets wagered. Very often, insiders have special knowledge of who may emerge victorious, and with this knowledge they will win more than they lose over a period of time. Likewise, those who gamble with the least amount of knowledge are destined to lose over a period of time.

The stock market (and investment markets in general) works in a similar fashion. Companies which are deemed superior are afforded greater price-earnings (P/E) and price-sales (P/S) multiples by the marketplace, which in effect level the playing field. Over the years, I have taken to using the price sales ratio as a more meaningful number than the price earnings ratio, although they should generally both be used, along with cash flow, enterprise value and a host of other numbers. For simplicity's sake let's compare the P/S for Toyota and GM. Toyota's P/S is greater than one. GM's P/S is closer to zero. This is telling us that Toyota is the much safer bet, but at the same time, if GM can get its house in order, the potential payoff may be huge. We could take another example in which the competitors are more closely matched. A good example would be Dell and Hewlett Packard. Dell's P/S recently came down from about 2 to 1.2, while Hewlett's climbed in recent years from about 0.25 to 1. During these moves, Dell's stock price dropped approximately 30% while Hewlett's rose about 200%. Clearly the smart money was on Hewlett. But now that the P/S ratios are in a tighter range, it will be interesting to see how things turn out. My personal belief is that each of these companies has achieved a natural P/S for itself, and we won't see much change in these levels for the foreseeable future. Where they stand now, Dell is still the favored company, and as such, the market has assigned it a higher P/S to level the playing field. As in the gambling scenario, the smart money had better information and was therefore able to capitalize on the disparity between the two stocks, and of course the "bookies" (brokers, advisers, money managers, real estate brokers, etc.) took their cuts as well. The loser, once again, was the less informed investor.

The Pious Man

I have heard a story several times over the years, told by different rabbis. I have taken it to heart, and I have often shared it with friends and relatives when I am trying to make a point. I want to share this story with you.

There was a great flood, and the local community was being evacuated for the safety of the residents. There was a religious man who had compete faith in god, and had complete faith that god would save him. He chose not to evacuate when the rescuers came, but rather, to remain in his home with his wife. As the water level began rising and the couple climbed to the second story of their home, the rescue workers came by in a boat, and asked the man and his wife to come with them. The man declined and professed his faith in god. The water level rose further, and the man and his wife climbed to the roof of their house. Later, with the water level still rising, and the man and his wife clinging to their chimney, a helicopter came for them. "This is the last time we will be here to offer you a ride to safety", said the rescuer, as the helicopter flew away. Shortly thereafter the man and his wife drowned. The man, being among the most pious, ascended to heaven, and on his way there, he encountered god. He pleaded with god to know why god had abandoned him, and had left him and his wife to drown, after he had lived such a pious life. To this god responded that the man was a fool, and that in fact god had sent the rescue workers three times to save the man and his wife, and all three times the man refused to be saved.

I tell you this story because you are being given all the signs of the impending financial debacle to come, as you were given in 2000, and if you are like most people, you are still refusing to observe the signals. Don't be like the man who drowned.

Summary

Imagine the investment markets as a single life; your life. You have many components to your life which make you whole. These are your family, your health, your finances, your work, your hobbies, etc. At various points in your life, some of these things are going well, some not so well, some are neglected and some get extra attention. At certain times, you have no choice (i.e. emergencies, health, financial problems, etc.), and you must neglect certain areas. At other times, everything can be going extraordinarily well. But you know this probably won't last, because it never does. And when one area gets too much attention, it's usually time to reallocate your time and energy to the other areas to ensure more balance.

The investment markets are going through a rare moment where everything is firing away. Real estate, stocks, bonds, and commodities are all going gangbusters, so we have to ask ourselves whether we truly believe this can last. We know from experience that it never does. Therefore, every reader should act to rebalance their investments in much the same way they would ideally be rebalancing their lives. This means more cash (safe money markets and treasuries).

Remember! Don't listen to the "experts", because many of them are not truly experts, many of them do not truly have your interests at heart, and/or many of them are not truthful.

ABOUT THE AUTHOR

Fred Press began actively investing in the 1970's. He graduated from Stevens Institute of Technology with a degree in mechanical engineering, and earned a master's in mechanical engineering while teaching thermodynamics at Drexel University on full scholarship. This real-life "rocket scientist" then went to work for General Electric, designing aircraft engines while he completed his MBA in the Boston University evening program. During the 1980's, he researched options strategies, utilized hedging techniques in the midst of the 1987 crash, and visited "floors" of Asian exchanges.

In the 1990's Fred went to work for a major Wall Street firm (where he scored in the top percentile on the industry standard Series 7 Exam) and was a one time instructor on investing for the Learning Annex in New York City. He left Wall Street to concentrate on his businesses, and on his investing and research. He has spent tens of thousands of hours developing his skills as an expert in data analysis and pattern recognition as applied to the "investment markets". There are few who possess his level of breadth, depth, and expertise in understanding the markets' inner workings.

For additional information, please go to fredpress.com or whatgreenspancant-tellyou.com.

Index

978-0-595-48283-
0-595-48283-X

www.ingramcontent.com/pod-product-compliance
Lightning Source LLC
Chambersburg PA
CBHW031050180526
45163CB00002BA/767